matthew

the gospel according to

matthew

authorised king james version

printed by authority

published by canongate

---

with an introduction by | a n wilson

First published in Great Britain in 1998
by Canongate Books Ltd
14 High Street, Edinburgh EH1 1TE

10 9 8 7 6 5 4 3 2

Introduction copyright © A N Wilson 1998
The moral right of the author has been asserted

British Library Cataloguing-in-Publication Data
A catalogue record is available on request from
the British Library

ISBN 0 86241 795 3

Typeset by Palimpsest Book Production
Book design by Paddy Cramsie
Printed and bound in Great Britain
by Caledonian International, Bishopbriggs

a note about pocket canons

The Authorised King James Version of the Bible, translated between 1603–11, coincided with an extraordinary flowering of English literature. This version, more than any other, and possibly more than any other work in history, has had an influence in shaping the language we speak and write today. Presenting individual books from the Bible as separate volumes, as they were originally conceived, encourages the reader to approach them as literary works in their own right.

The first twelve books in this series encompass categories as diverse as history, fiction, philosophy, love poetry and law. Each Pocket Canon also has its own introduction, specially commissioned from an impressive range of writers, which provides a personal interpretation of the text and explores its contemporary relevance.

A N Wilson is an award-winning novelist and biographer. He is the author of the best-selling Jesus *(1992) and* Paul: The Mind of the Apostle *(1997). His novels include* The Healing Art *(Somerset Maugham Award),* Wise Virgin *(W H Smith Award) and the five books in the* Lampitt Chronicles. *His biographies include studies of Sir Walter Scott, John Milton, Tolstoy, C S Lewis and Hillaire Belloc. He lives in north London.*

introduction by a n wilson

You are holding in your hands a tiny book which has changed more human lives than *The Communist Manifesto* or Freud's *Interpretation of Dreams*: a book which has shaped whole civilizations: a book which, for many people, has been not a gospel but The Gospel.

And you are bound to ask, because you are born out of time in a post-Christian age, into a world of newspapers and investigative reporting and science – 'Is it true?'

Did a Virgin really conceive (1:23) and give birth to a boy-child in Bethlehem (2:1)? Did wise men, guided by a star, come to worship him (2:2)? Did he grow up to be able to walk on water (14:26), to perform miracles, to found the Church (16:26), to rise from the dead?

Stop, stop. Don't ask. They are all questions which seem reasonable enough, but they will lead you into the most pointless, arid negativism. Your educated, scientific, modern mind will decide that no one ever walked on water; no Virgin ever conceived; that corpses do not come to life. And by rejecting this Gospel, you will reject one of the most disturbing and extraordinary books ever written; not, as you might think, on intelligent grounds, but because you (and I, alas) are too hemmed in by our imaginative limitations to see the sort of things this book is doing.

Before you apply to it the supposedly rational tests which you would apply to a newspaper report or a television documentary, imagine the chapters which describe the trial and Crucifixion of Christ set to music in Bach's *Saint Matthew Passion*. Consider the millions of people who, for the last 1900 years have recited the prayer (6:9–13) which begins 'Our Father'. Think of the old women in Stalin's Russia, when the men were too cowardly to profess their loyalty to the Church, who stubbornly continued to chant the opening verses of the Sermon on the Mount in defiance of the KGB. 'Blessed are they that mourn for they shall be comforted' (5:4).

This is a book, not of easily-dismissed fairy tales but of power and passion; more arresting, disturbing and truthful than most reading-matter which you could buy for the price of a magazine on a station bookstall or in the paperback store. This is the Gospel of Christ, in all its terribleness, its wonder, its awe-inspiring truth and its self-contradictions.

Nor should you think that the contradictory emotions which assail and trouble you as you read it – as trouble you they must – are all storms and tempest inside *you*. For this book itself was born out of conflict and struggle and contradiction.

Matthew's Gospel reflects the tension which saw the new religion – what we call Christianity – being fashioned from the old – Judaism. It is by paradox an intensely Jewish, and an intensely anti-Jewish work – indeed it is the great Ur-text of anti-semitism. The historical Jesus is not to be found in this book, nor in any book. He eludes our search. Matthew's Jesus is seen through the prism of a particular faith, of a particular group, somewhere in the Mediterranean world. Rome? 85–100 AD?

By the time the book reached something like its present form (50 years after Jesus had left the scene?) Christianity was emerging as something which, if not distinct from Judaism, was at least repellent to most Jews. Paul's Letter to the Galatians (of *circa* 50 AD) describes a rift between the first Christians of Asia Minor, converts of Paul, and the followers of Peter and James in Jerusalem who had known the earthly Jesus. It seems like an angry and irreconcilable quarrel. Paul, though, or because, a Jew, had decided that those who followed the Jewish Law (*Torah*), the Law given by God on Mount Sinai to his people, were living in bonds from which Christ came to set them free. For Peter and his friends, the dietary laws of Judaism, the requirement of circumcision, and so forth, were 'not bonds but wings'; they were symbols of lives dedicated to God.

No compromise, surely, was possible, between these two ways? Either you circumcise your son or you don't. Either it is sinful to eat pork, or it isn't.

But to another generation, Matthew's, the problems were different. The irreconcilables, rather than being fudged, are held together in self-contradiction. Peter and Paul, who in earlier New Testament texts were the leaders of opposing Ways, emerge in this text as co-partners (though, of course, Paul's ideas, rather than his name, are what we find here).

It is Jesus himself, in this legendary reconstruction, who speaks lines which, in an earlier generation of Christianity, had been assigned to protagonists in the quarrel. On the one hand, with the followers of Paul, he wants to leave the synagogue. See chapter 12, a key moment, when the Pharisees accuse Jesus of breaking the Law by healing a man on the Sabbath. His reaction is to lead his people away from the mainstream of Jewry, but he does so, as Paul had done, by quoting the Jewish Scriptures. 'I will put my spirit upon him, and he shall shew judgment to the Gentiles' (12:18). On the other hand, Matthew's Jesus is not simply a libertarian like Paul. He wishes to reassure the Jewish conservatives: 'Think not that I am come to destroy the law, or the prophets: I am not come to destroy, but to fulfil' (5:17).

How is the miracle accomplished? It is done by seeing the new congregation or synagogue, or gathering-together of the Elect as the New Israel: the Church.

So Matthew constructs his book as a miniature *Torah*. Like Moses, Matthew's Jesus goes up to a mountain (5:1) and delivers a New Law to his followers. At the end of the tale, in a gesture which could never have taken place in history but which is heavy with religious paradox, a pagan, Roman Governor performs a Jewish purification ritual – he washes his hands – to demonstrate his innocence of Christ's murder. It is the Jewish mob who cry out, 'His blood be on us, and on our children' (27:25). A terrible text which would have profound consequences in Europe during the centuries that it penetrated the collective consciousness. It was not just a few Jews in this Gospel who are responsible for the torture and death of Jesus. It is 'all the people' (27:25).

Matthew's Gospel is not just the product of the embryo-Church. It is, really, a book about the Church, and it shapes what the Church, both in East and West, was destined to become.

The Church is a house founded upon a rock; and that rock is, primarily, the teaching of Christ. 'Therefore, whosoever heareth these sayings of mine, and doeth them, I will liken him unto a wise man, which built his house upon a rock: and the rain descended, and the floods came, and the winds blew, and beat upon that house; and it fell not: for it was founded upon a rock' (7:24–5).

The teachings, of course, are the exact reverse of worldly-wise notions of security. Our obsessions with security – financial, military, domestic – are blown sky high by Jesus's teaching: not to lay up treasure, not to resist evil with violence. Yet a detachment from what we would call security seems like a prerequisite here for church membership. And the Church, for Matthew, is the ante-chamber of the Kingdom of God.

And notice the extraordinary emphasis on the superiority of the poor over the rich. When John the Baptist asks (chapter 11) whether Jesus is the One who is to come, the message comes back, 'Go and shew John again those things which ye do hear and see'. A list follows, reaching a rhetorical *crescendo*. 'The blind receive their sight, and the lame walk, the lepers are cleansed, and the deaf hear, the dead are raised up' … Each thing is more remarkable than the last. But what is more remarkable even than the resurrection of the dead? The final item in the list: 'The poor have the gospel preached to them' (11:4–5).

That is not because Jesus was a sentimentalist or a socialist. It is because only the detached and the dispossessed, that is the poor, can hear his gospel. When a rich young man tried to follow Jesus, he 'went away sorrowful' (19:22) because the message was too simple, and too stern. Only those who live as though there is no tomorrow, and who do not store up treasure, can enter the kingdom.

This is the rock on which the Church is founded. It is founded on a rock in another sense: it is founded on Simon whose title or nickname, given to him by Jesus in one of the most dramatic scenes in the Gospel, is Peter. There is no name 'Peter' in the ancient world. You find it on no ossuary or tomb. It is a word meaning 'Rock'. It is a Gospel word. In chapter 16, Jesus asks his friends who do men say that he is? And they tell him – some say he is a prophet, or Elijah come back to earth. But you? Who do you say that he is?

The fisherman from Galilee blurts out, '"Thou art the Christ, the Son of the Living God." And Jesus answered and said unto him, "Blessed art thou, Simon Bar-Jona: for flesh and blood hath not revealed it unto thee, but my Father which is in heaven. And I say unto thee, that thou art Peter, and upon this rock I will build my church;' (16:16–18).

This is the Simon who, only a little while earlier (14:27–31) has attempted to walk with Jesus on the water of the stormy lake of Galilee and who has sunk because he had no faith. This is the Simon Peter who, as Jesus had predicted, has no courage at the last. As Jesus had predicted, when his Master had been arrested, Peter denies even knowing him; and, when he confronts his own cowardice and weakness, 'he went out and wept bitterly' (26:75).

Here we see how the Christian community which shaped

this Gospel has reconciled the early conflicts between Paul – for whom the Gospel was the acceptance of Grace – and Peter for whom it had been an observance of Law. For the Rock on which the Church is founded is not a rock of success, or moral strength, but of doubt, weakness, failure. The boat (another metaphor for the Church throughout this book) runs into storms and its crew panics. Only Jesus, apparently asleep, can calm the storms. 'And he hath said unto me, "My grace is sufficient for thee, for my strength is made perfect in weakness".' (2 *Corinthians* 12:9).

The attempt to follow the new *Torah*, the Sermon on the Mount, will not lead to a new legalism. Nor will anyone be able to follow Jesus's command to be perfect, even as God is perfect (5:48). Instead, it will lead to an understanding that, though we might abstain from murder, we shall still be angry; though we might avoid adultery, that is nothing to be proud of: for we shall still feel lust. It is Matthew the sinner and tax gatherer who is accepted in the Beloved. Christ the physician comes to heal sinners, not the righteous.

The author of this book did not attempt to write a realistic narrative of the kind we might expect from a post-enlightenment historian. For instance, judging from the earliest Christian writings and the *Letters of Paul*, it seems fairly likely that the Church began in Jerusalem. But *Matthew* has it beginning on a hillside in Galilee. *Mark*, the Gospel on which this book relies so heavily, says nothing about a miraculous conception, or a birth in Bethlehem. But the tale of a Virgin-birth and the recognition of the child by the wise men from the east perfectly illustrates the double-sided purpose of this book. On the one hand, the child is born to fulfil the Messianic prophecies of Judaism. On the other hand, he is recognised, not by the king of the Jews, but by wise Gentiles. Just so, at the end, he tells his followers to go into the ends of the earth, baptizing and teaching all people.

The sceptical mind will find these 28 chapters to be a catalogue of improbabilities. To any student of ethics, who has studied Aristotle or John Stuart Mill, or Dewey or Rawls, here is no morality at all but what Chesterton called 'The Ethics of Elfland'.

At the centre-stage is Jesus, calling the rich to discard their wealth and offering the kingdom to the poor. He offers not peace but a sword (10:34). Yet he says (11:28), 'Come unto me, all ye that labour and are heavy laden, and I will give you rest.'

Perhaps the most distinctive and haunting of all Matthew's stories – perhaps the most haunting passage in the entire New Testament – is that parable in the final discourse (25:31–46) when Jesus predicts that the King will welcome the chosen into his kingdom. They are those who have seen him, not in his glory, but as poor, naked, hungry, in prison and in need. Neither the blessed, nor the damned, in this tale, understand during their lifetimes, that in so far as they responded to the depths of human need in others, they had responded to God. It is in the context of this story that we begin to understand the sense in which this book is true. By the stern test of that parable and of this Gospel, most of us will feel like that rich young man. We will go away sorrowful, deeply conscious of our inability either to understand the Gospel, or to live up to its precepts or to have the humility to accept Divine Grace. Yet, though we are sorrowful, and though we go away, we shall never read this text without being, in some small degree, changed.

the gospel according to st matthew

The book of the generation of Jesus Christ, the son of David, the son of Abraham.

²Abraham begat Isaac; and Isaac begat Jacob; and Jacob begat Judas and his brethren. ³And Judas begat Phares and Zara of Thamar; and Phares begat Esrom; and Esrom begat Aram. ⁴And Aram begat Aminadab; and Aminadab begat Naasson; and Naasson begat Salmon. ⁵And Salmon begat Booz of Rachab; and Booz begat Obed of Ruth; and Obed begat Jesse. ⁶And Jesse begat David the king; and David the king begat Solomon of her that had been the wife of Urias. ⁷And Solomon begat Roboam; and Roboam begat Abia; and Abia begat Asa. ⁸And Asa begat Josaphat; and Josaphat begat Joram; and Joram begat Ozias. ⁹And Ozias begat Joatham; and Joatham begat Achaz; and Achaz begat Ezekias. ¹⁰And Ezekias begat Manasses; and Manasses begat Amon; and Amon begat Josias. ¹¹And Josias begat Jechonias and his brethren, about the time they were carried away to Babylon. ¹²And after they were brought to Babylon, Jechonias begat Salathiel; and Salathiel begat Zorobabel. ¹³And Zorobabel begat Abiud; and Abiud begat Eliakim; and Eliakim begat Azor. ¹⁴And Azor begat Sadoc; and Sadoc begat Achim; and Achim begat Eliud. ¹⁵And Eliud begat Eleazar; and Eleazar begat Matthan; and Matthan begat Jacob. ¹⁶And Jacob begat Joseph the

husband of Mary, of whom was born Jesus, who is called Christ. ¹⁷ So all the generations from Abraham to David are fourteen generations; and from David until the carrying away into Babylon are fourteen generations; and from the carrying away into Babylon unto Christ are fourteen generations.

¹⁸ Now the birth of Jesus Christ was on this wise. When as his mother Mary was espoused to Joseph, before they came together, she was found with child of the Holy Ghost. ¹⁹ Then Joseph her husband, being a just man, and not willing to make her a publick example, was minded to put her away privily. ²⁰ But while he thought on these things, behold, the angel of the Lord appeared unto him in a dream, saying, 'Joseph, thou son of David, fear not to take unto thee Mary thy wife, for that which is conceived in her is of the Holy Ghost. ²¹ And she shall bring forth a son, and thou shalt call his name "Jesus": for he shall save his people from their sins.' ²² Now all this was done, that it might be fulfilled which was spoken of the Lord by the prophet, saying, ²³ 'Behold, a virgin shall be with child, and shall bring forth a son, and they shall call his name "Emmanuel", which being interpreted is, "God with us". ²⁴ Then Joseph being raised from sleep did as the angel of the Lord had bidden him, and took unto him his wife; ²⁵ and knew her not till she had brought forth her firstborn son, and he called his name 'Jesus'.

2 Now when Jesus was born in Bethlehem of Judæa in the days of Herod the king, behold, there came wise men from the east to Jerusalem, ² saying, 'Where is he that is born King of the Jews? For we have seen his star in the east, and

are come to worship him.' ³When Herod the king had heard these things, he was troubled, and all Jerusalem with him. ⁴And when he had gathered all the chief priests and scribes of the people together, he demanded of them where Christ should be born. ⁵And they said unto him, 'In Bethlehem of Judæa, for thus it is written by the prophet, ⁶"And thou Bethlehem, in the land of Juda, art not the least among the princes of Juda, for out of thee shall come a Governor, that shall rule my people Israel."' ⁷Then Herod, when he had privily called the wise men, enquired of them diligently what time the star appeared. ⁸And he sent them to Bethlehem, and said, 'Go and search diligently for the young child; and when ye have found him, bring me word again, that I may come and worship him also.' ⁹When they had heard the king, they departed; and, lo, the star, which they saw in the east, went before them, till it came and stood over where the young child was. ¹⁰When they saw the star, they rejoiced with exceeding great joy.

¹¹And when they were come into the house, they saw the young child with Mary his mother, and fell down, and worshipped him, and when they had opened their treasures, they presented unto him gifts: gold, and frankincense, and myrrh. ¹²And being warned of God in a dream that they should not return to Herod, they departed into their own country another way. ¹³And when they were departed, behold, the angel of the Lord appeareth to Joseph in a dream, saying, 'Arise, and take the young child and his mother, and flee into Egypt, and be thou there until I bring thee word, for Herod will seek the young child to destroy him.' ¹⁴When he arose, he

took the young child and his mother by night, and departed into Egypt, ¹⁵ and was there until the death of Herod, that it might be fulfilled which was spoken of the Lord by the prophet, saying, 'Out of Egypt have I called my son.'

¹⁶ Then Herod, when he saw that he was mocked of the wise men, was exceeding wroth, and sent forth, and slew all the children that were in Bethlehem, and in all the coasts thereof, from two years old and under, according to the time which he had diligently enquired of the wise men. ¹⁷ Then was fulfilled that which was spoken by Jeremy the prophet, saying, ¹⁸ 'In Rama was there a voice heard, lamentation, and weeping, and great mourning, Rachel weeping for her children, and would not be comforted, because they are not.'

¹⁹ But when Herod was dead, behold, an angel of the Lord appeareth in a dream to Joseph in Egypt, ²⁰ saying, 'Arise, and take the young child and his mother, and go into the land of Israel, for they are dead which sought the young child's life.' ²¹ And he arose, and took the young child and his mother, and came into the land of Israel. ²² But when he heard that Archelaus did reign in Judæa in the room of his father Herod, he was afraid to go thither; notwithstanding, being warned of God in a dream, he turned aside into the parts of Galilee. ²³ And he came and dwelt in a city called Nazareth, that it might be fulfilled which was spoken by the prophets, 'He shall be called a Nazarene.'

3 In those days came John the Baptist, preaching in the wilderness of Judæa, ² and saying, 'Repent ye, for the kingdom of heaven is at hand.' ³ For this is he that was spoken

of by the prophet Esaias, saying, 'The voice of one crying in the wilderness, "Prepare ye the way of the Lord, make his paths straight."' ⁴And the same John had his raiment of camel's hair, and a leathern girdle about his loins; and his meat was locusts and wild honey. ⁵Then went out to him Jerusalem, and all Judæa, and all the region round about Jordan, ⁶and were baptized of him in Jordan, confessing their sins.

⁷But when he saw many of the Pharisees and Sadducees come to his baptism, he said unto them, 'O generation of vipers, who hath warned you to flee from the wrath to come? ⁸Bring forth therefore fruits meet for repentance, ⁹and think not to say within yourselves, "We have Abraham to our father," for I say unto you that God is able of these stones to raise up children unto Abraham. ¹⁰And now also the axe is laid unto the root of the trees: therefore every tree which bringeth not forth good fruit is hewn down, and cast into the fire. ¹¹I indeed baptize you with water unto repentance, but he that cometh after me is mightier than I, whose shoes I am not worthy to bear. He shall baptize you with the Holy Ghost, and with fire, ¹²whose fan is in his hand, and he will throughly purge his floor, and gather his wheat into the garner; but he will burn up the chaff with unquenchable fire.'

¹³Then cometh Jesus from Galilee to Jordan unto John, to be baptized of him. ¹⁴But John forbad him, saying, 'I have need to be baptized of thee, and comest thou to me?' ¹⁵And Jesus answering said unto him, 'Suffer it to be so now, for thus it becometh us to fulfil all righteousness.' Then he suffered him. ¹⁶And Jesus, when he was baptized, went up straightway out of the water, and, lo, the heavens were opened unto

him, and he saw the Spirit of God descending like a dove, and lighting upon him: ¹⁷and lo a voice from heaven, saying, 'This is my beloved Son, in whom I am well pleased.'

4 Then was Jesus led up of the Spirit into the wilderness to be tempted of the devil. ²And when he had fasted forty days and forty nights, he was afterward an hungred. ³And when the tempter came to him, he said, 'If thou be the Son of God, command that these stones be made bread.' ⁴But he answered and said, 'It is written, "Man shall not live by bread alone, but by every word that proceedeth out of the mouth of God."' ⁵Then the devil taketh him up into the holy city, and setteth him on a pinnacle of the temple, ⁶and saith unto him, 'If thou be the Son of God, cast thyself down, for it is written, "He shall give his angels charge concerning thee, and in their hands they shall bear thee up, lest at any time thou dash thy foot against a stone."' ⁷Jesus said unto him, 'It is written again, "Thou shalt not tempt the Lord thy God."' ⁸Again, the devil taketh him up into an exceeding high mountain, and sheweth him all the kingdoms of the world, and the glory of them; ⁹and saith unto him, 'All these things will I give thee, if thou wilt fall down and worship me.' ¹⁰Then saith Jesus unto him, 'Get thee hence, Satan: for it is written, "Thou shalt worship the Lord thy God, and him only shalt thou serve."' ¹¹Then the devil leaveth him, and, behold, angels came and ministered unto him.

¹²Now when Jesus had heard that John was cast into prison, he departed into Galilee; ¹³and leaving Nazareth, he came and dwelt in Capernaum, which is upon the sea coast,

in the borders of Zabulon and Nephthalim, ¹⁴ that it might be fulfilled which was spoken by Esaias the prophet, saying, ¹⁵ 'The land of Zabulon, and the land of Nephthalim, by the way of the sea, beyond Jordan, Galilee of the Gentiles; ¹⁶ the people which sat in darkness saw great light; and to them which sat in the region and shadow of death light is sprung up.'

¹⁷ From that time Jesus began to preach, and to say, 'Repent, for the kingdom of heaven is at hand.'

¹⁸ And Jesus, walking by the sea of Galilee, saw two brethren, Simon called Peter, and Andrew his brother, casting a net into the sea, for they were fishers. ¹⁹ And he saith unto them, 'Follow me, and I will make you fishers of men.' ²⁰ And they straightway left their nets, and followed him. ²¹ And going on from thence, he saw other two brethren, James the son of Zebedee, and John his brother, in a ship with Zebedee their father, mending their nets; and he called them. ²² And they immediately left the ship and their father, and followed him.

²³ And Jesus went about all Galilee, teaching in their synagogues, and preaching the gospel of the kingdom, and healing all manner of sickness and all manner of disease among the people. ²⁴ And his fame went throughout all Syria, and they brought unto him all sick people that were taken with divers diseases and torments, and those which were possessed with devils, and those which were lunatick, and those that had the palsy; and he healed them. ²⁵ And there followed him great multitudes of people from Galilee, and from Decapolis, and from Jerusalem, and from Judæa, and from beyond Jordan.

5 And seeing the multitudes, he went up into a mountain, and when he was set, his disciples came unto him, ²and he opened his mouth, and taught them, saying,

> ³ Blessed are the poor in spirit,
>> for theirs is the kingdom of heaven.
> ⁴ Blessed are they that mourn,
>> for they shall be comforted.
> ⁵ Blessed are the meek,
>> for they shall inherit the earth.
> ⁶ Blessed are they which do hunger
>> and thirst after righteousness,
>>> for they shall be filled.
> ⁷ Blessed are the merciful,
>> for they shall obtain mercy.
> ⁸ Blessed are the pure in heart,
>> for they shall see God.
> ⁹ Blessed are the peacemakers,
>> for they shall be called the children of God.
> ¹⁰ Blessed are they which are persecuted
>> for righteousness' sake,
>>> for theirs is the kingdom of heaven.
> ¹¹ Blessed are ye, when men shall revile you,
>> and persecute you, and shall say all manner
>>> of evil against you falsely, for my sake.

¹²'Rejoice, and be exceeding glad, for great is your reward in heaven, for so persecuted they the prophets which were before you.

¹³'Ye are the salt of the earth: but if the salt have lost his

savour, wherewith shall it be salted? It is thenceforth good for nothing, but to be cast out, and to be trodden under foot of men. ¹⁴ Ye are the light of the world. A city that is set on an hill cannot be hid. ¹⁵ Neither do men light a candle, and put it under a bushel, but on a candlestick; and it giveth light unto all that are in the house. ¹⁶ Let your light so shine before men, that they may see your good works, and glorify your Father which is in heaven.

¹⁷ 'Think not that I am come to destroy the law, or the prophets; I am not come to destroy, but to fulfil. ¹⁸ For verily I say unto you, till heaven and earth pass, one jot or one tittle shall in no wise pass from the law, till all be fulfilled. ¹⁹ Whosoever therefore shall break one of these least commandments, and shall teach men so, he shall be called the least in the kingdom of heaven: but whosoever shall do and teach them, the same shall be called great in the kingdom of heaven. ²⁰ For I say unto you that, except your righteousness shall exceed the righteousness of the scribes and Pharisees, ye shall in no case enter into the kingdom of heaven.

²¹ 'Ye have heard that it was said by them of old time, "Thou shalt not kill", and whosoever shall kill shall be in danger of the judgment: ²² but I say unto you that whosoever is angry with his brother without a cause shall be in danger of the judgment, and whosoever shall say to his brother, "Raca," shall be in danger of the council, but whosoever shall say, "Thou fool," shall be in danger of hell fire. ²³ Therefore if thou bring thy gift to the altar, and there rememberest that thy brother hath ought against thee, ²⁴ leave there thy gift before the altar, and go thy way; first be reconciled to

thy brother, and then come and offer thy gift. ²⁵Agree with thine adversary quickly, whiles thou art in the way with him; lest at any time the adversary deliver thee to the judge, and the judge deliver thee to the officer, and thou be cast into prison. ²⁶Verily I say unto thee, thou shalt by no means come out thence, till thou hast paid the uttermost farthing.

²⁷'Ye have heard that it was said by them of old time, "Thou shalt not commit adultery," ²⁸but I say unto you that whosoever looketh on a woman to lust after her hath committed adultery with her already in his heart. ²⁹And if thy right eye offend thee, pluck it out, and cast it from thee: for it is profitable for thee that one of thy members should perish, and not that thy whole body should be cast into hell. ³⁰And if thy right hand offend thee, cut it off, and cast it from thee: for it is profitable for thee that one of thy members should perish, and not that thy whole body should be cast into hell. ³¹It hath been said, "Whosoever shall put away his wife, let him give her a writing of divorcement." ³²But I say unto you that whosoever shall put away his wife, saving for the cause of fornication, causeth her to commit adultery, and whosoever shall marry her that is divorced committeth adultery.

³³'Again, ye have heard that it hath been said by them of old time, "Thou shalt not forswear thyself, but shalt perform unto the Lord thine oaths." ³⁴But I say unto you, "Swear not at all; neither by heaven, for it is God's throne, ³⁵nor by the earth, for it is his footstool, neither by Jerusalem, for it is the city of the great King." ³⁶Neither shalt thou swear by thy head, because thou canst not make one hair white or black. ³⁷But let your communication be "Yea, yea", "Nay, nay", for

whatsoever is more than these cometh of evil.

³⁸ 'Ye have heard that it hath been said, "An eye for an eye, and a tooth for a tooth": ³⁹ but I say unto you that ye resist not evil, but whosoever shall smite thee on thy right cheek, turn to him the other also. ⁴⁰And if any man will sue thee at the law, and take away thy coat, let him have thy cloke also. ⁴¹And whosoever shall compel thee to go a mile, go with him twain. ⁴² Give to him that asketh thee, and from him that would borrow of thee turn not thou away.

⁴³ 'Ye have heard that it hath been said, "Thou shalt love thy neighbour, and hate thine enemy." ⁴⁴ But I say unto you, "Love your enemies, bless them that curse you, do good to them that hate you, and pray for them which despitefully use you, and persecute you"; ⁴⁵ that ye may be the children of your Father which is in heaven, for he maketh his sun to rise on the evil and on the good, and sendeth rain on the just and on the unjust. ⁴⁶ For if ye love them which love you, what reward have ye? Do not even the publicans the same? ⁴⁷ And if ye salute your brethren only, what do ye more than others? Do not even the publicans so? ⁴⁸ Be ye therefore perfect, even as your Father which is in heaven is perfect.

6 'Take heed that ye do not your alms before men, to be seen of them; otherwise ye have no reward of your Father which is in heaven. ² Therefore when thou doest thine alms, do not sound a trumpet before thee, as the hypocrites do in the synagogues and in the streets, that they may have glory of men. Verily I say unto you, "They have their reward." ³ But when thou doest alms, let not thy left hand know what thy right hand doeth, [4] that thine alms may be in secret, and thy Father which seeth in secret himself shall reward thee openly.

[5] 'And when thou prayest, thou shalt not be as the hypocrites are, for they love to pray standing in the synagogues and in the corners of the streets, that they may be seen of men. Verily I say unto you, "They have their reward." [6] But thou, when thou prayest, enter into thy closet, and when thou hast shut thy door, pray to thy Father which is in secret; and thy Father which seeth in secret shall reward thee openly. [7] But when ye pray, use not vain repetitions, as the heathen do, for they think that they shall be heard for their much speaking. [8] Be not ye therefore like unto them, for your Father knoweth what things ye have need of, before ye ask him. [9] After this manner therefore pray ye:

> Our Father which art in heaven,
>> Hallowed be thy name.
> [10] Thy kingdom come.
>> Thy will be done in earth, as it is in heaven.
> [11] Give us this day our daily bread.
> [12] And forgive us our debts,
>> as we forgive our debtors.
> [13] And lead us not into temptation,
>> but deliver us from evil:
>>> for thine is the kingdom,
>> and the power, and the glory,
>>> for ever. Amen.

[14] 'For if ye forgive men their trespasses, your heavenly Father will also forgive you, [15] but if ye forgive not men their

trespasses, neither will your Father forgive your trespasses.

¹⁶ 'Moreover when ye fast, be not, as the hypocrites, of a sad countenance: for they disfigure their faces, that they may appear unto men to fast. Verily I say unto you, "They have their reward." ¹⁷ But thou, when thou fastest, anoint thine head, and wash thy face, ¹⁸ that thou appear not unto men to fast, but unto thy Father which is in secret: and thy Father, which seeth in secret, shall reward thee openly.

¹⁹ 'Lay not up for yourselves treasures upon earth, where moth and rust doth corrupt, and where thieves break through and steal, ²⁰ but lay up for yourselves treasures in heaven, where neither moth nor rust doth corrupt, and where thieves do not break through nor steal: ²¹ for where your treasure is, there will your heart be also. ²² The light of the body is the eye: if therefore thine eye be single, thy whole body shall be full of light. ²³ But if thine eye be evil, thy whole body shall be full of darkness. If therefore the light that is in thee be darkness, how great is that darkness!

²⁴ 'No man can serve two masters: for either he will hate the one, and love the other; or else he will hold to the one, and despise the other. Ye cannot serve God and mammon. ²⁵ Therefore I say unto you, take no thought for your life, what ye shall eat, or what ye shall drink; nor yet for your body, what ye shall put on. Is not the life more than meat, and the body than raiment? ²⁶ Behold the fowls of the air, for they sow not, neither do they reap, nor gather into barns; yet your heavenly Father feedeth them. Are ye not much better than they? ²⁷ Which of you by taking thought can add one cubit unto his stature? ²⁸ And why take ye thought for

raiment? Consider the lilies of the field, how they grow; they toil not, neither do they spin, ²⁹ and yet I say unto you that even Solomon in all his glory was not arrayed like one of these. ³⁰ Wherefore, if God so clothe the grass of the field, which today is, and tomorrow is cast into the oven, shall he not much more clothe you, O ye of little faith? ³¹ Therefore take no thought, saying, "What shall we eat?" or, "What shall we drink?" or, "Wherewithal shall we be clothed?" ³²(For after all these things do the Gentiles seek) for your heavenly Father knoweth that ye have need of all these things. ³³ But seek ye first the kingdom of God, and his righteousness; and all these things shall be added unto you. ³⁴ Take therefore no thought for the morrow, for the morrow shall take thought for the things of itself. Sufficient unto the day is the evil thereof.

7 'Judge not, that ye be not judged. ² For with what judgment ye judge, ye shall be judged, and with what measure ye mete, it shall be measured to you again. ³ And why beholdest thou the mote that is in thy brother's eye, but considerest not the beam that is in thine own eye? ⁴ Or how wilt thou say to thy brother, "Let me pull out the mote out of thine eye," and, behold, a beam is in thine own eye? ⁵ Thou hypocrite, first cast out the beam out of thine own eye; and then shalt thou see clearly to cast out the mote out of thy brother's eye.

⁶ 'Give not that which is holy unto the dogs, neither cast ye your pearls before swine, lest they trample them under their feet, and turn again and rend you.

⁷ 'Ask, and it shall be given you; seek, and ye shall find;

knock, and it shall be opened unto you: ⁸ for every one that asketh receiveth; and he that seeketh findeth; and to him that knocketh it shall be opened. ⁹ Or what man is there of you, whom if his son ask bread, will he give him a stone? ¹⁰ Or if he ask a fish, will he give him a serpent? ¹¹ If ye then, being evil, know how to give good gifts unto your children, how much more shall your Father which is in heaven give good things to them that ask him? ¹² Therefore all things whatsoever ye would that men should do to you, do ye even so to them: for this is the law and the prophets.

¹³ 'Enter ye in at the strait gate, for wide is the gate, and broad is the way, that leadeth to destruction, and many there be which go in thereat. ¹⁴ Because strait is the gate, and narrow is the way, which leadeth unto life, and few there be that find it.

¹⁵ 'Beware of false prophets, which come to you in sheep's clothing, but inwardly they are ravening wolves. ¹⁶ Ye shall know them by their fruits. Do men gather grapes of thorns, or figs of thistles? ¹⁷ Even so every good tree bringeth forth good fruit; but a corrupt tree bringeth forth evil fruit. ¹⁸ A good tree cannot bring forth evil fruit, neither can a corrupt tree bring forth good fruit. ¹⁹ Every tree that bringeth not forth good fruit is hewn down, and cast into the fire. ²⁰ Wherefore by their fruits ye shall know them.

²¹ 'Not every one that saith unto me, "Lord, Lord," shall enter into the kingdom of heaven; but he that doeth the will of my Father which is in heaven. ²² Many will say to me in that day, "Lord, Lord, have we not prophesied in thy name? And in thy name have cast out devils? And in thy name done

many wonderful works?" ²³And then will I profess unto them, "I never knew you: depart from me, ye that work iniquity."

²⁴'Therefore whosoever heareth these sayings of mine, and doeth them, I will liken him unto a wise man, which built his house upon a rock: ²⁵and the rain descended, and the floods came, and the winds blew, and beat upon that house; and it fell not: for it was founded upon a rock. ²⁶And every one that heareth these sayings of mine, and doeth them not, shall be likened unto a foolish man, which built his house upon the sand, ²⁷and the rain descended, and the floods came, and the winds blew, and beat upon that house; and it fell, and great was the fall of it.' ²⁸And it came to pass, when Jesus had ended these sayings, the people were astonished at his doctrine: ²⁹for he taught them as one having authority, and not as the scribes.

8 When he was come down from the mountain, great multitudes followed him. ²And, behold, there came a leper and worshipped him, saying, 'Lord, if thou wilt, thou canst make me clean.' ³And Jesus put forth his hand, and touched him, saying, 'I will; be thou clean.' And immediately his leprosy was cleansed. ⁴And Jesus saith unto him, 'See thou tell no man; but go thy way, shew thyself to the priest, and offer the gift that Moses commanded, for a testimony unto them.'

⁵And when Jesus was entered into Capernaum, there came unto him a centurion, beseeching him, ⁶and saying, 'Lord, my servant lieth at home sick of the palsy, grievously tormented.' ⁷And Jesus saith unto him, 'I will come and heal

him.' ⁸ The centurion answered and said, 'Lord, I am not worthy that thou shouldest come under my roof: but speak the word only, and my servant shall be healed. ⁹ For I am a man under authority, having soldiers under me, and I say to this man, "Go," and he goeth; and to another, "Come," and he cometh; and to my servant, "Do this," and he doeth it.' ¹⁰ When Jesus heard it, he marvelled, and said to them that followed, 'Verily I say unto you, I have not found so great faith, no, not in Israel. ¹¹ And I say unto you that many shall come from the east and west, and shall sit down with Abraham, and Isaac, and Jacob, in the kingdom of heaven. ¹² But the children of the kingdom shall be cast out into outer darkness: there shall be weeping and gnashing of teeth.' ¹³ And Jesus said unto the centurion, 'Go thy way; and as thou hast believed, so be it done unto thee.' And his servant was healed in the selfsame hour.

¹⁴ And when Jesus was come into Peter's house, he saw his wife's mother laid, and sick of a fever. ¹⁵ And he touched her hand, and the fever left her, and she arose, and ministered unto them.

¹⁶ When the even was come, they brought unto him many that were possessed with devils, and he cast out the spirits with his word, and healed all that were sick, ¹⁷ that it might be fulfilled which was spoken by Esaias the prophet, saying, 'Himself took our infirmities, and bare our sicknesses.'

¹⁸ Now when Jesus saw great multitudes about him, he gave commandment to depart unto the other side. ¹⁹ And a certain scribe came, and said unto him, 'Master, I will follow thee whithersoever thou goest.' ²⁰ And Jesus saith unto him,

'The foxes have holes, and the birds of the air have nests; but the Son of man hath not where to lay his head.' ²¹And another of his disciples said unto him, 'Lord, suffer me first to go and bury my father.' ²²But Jesus said unto him, 'Follow me; and let the dead bury their dead.'

²³And when he was entered into a ship, his disciples followed him. ²⁴And, behold, there arose a great tempest in the sea, insomuch that the ship was covered with the waves; but he was asleep. ²⁵And his disciples came to him, and awoke him, saying, 'Lord, save us. We perish.' ²⁶And he saith unto them, 'Why are ye fearful, O ye of little faith?' Then he arose, and rebuked the winds and the sea; and there was a great calm. ²⁷But the men marvelled, saying, 'What manner of man is this, that even the winds and the sea obey him!'

²⁸And when he was come to the other side into the country of the Gergesenes, there met him two possessed with devils, coming out of the tombs, exceeding fierce, so that no man might pass by that way. ²⁹And, behold, they cried out, saying, 'What have we to do with thee, Jesus, thou Son of God? Art thou come hither to torment us before the time?' ³⁰And there was a good way off from them an herd of many swine feeding. ³¹So the devils besought him, saying, 'If thou cast us out, suffer us to go away into the herd of swine.' ³²And he said unto them, 'Go.' And when they were come out, they went into the herd of swine, and, behold, the whole herd of swine ran violently down a steep place into the sea, and perished in the waters. ³³And they that kept them fled, and went their ways into the city, and told every thing, and what was befallen to the possessed of the devils. ³⁴And,

behold, the whole city came out to meet Jesus, and when they saw him, they besought him that he would depart out of their coasts.

9 And he entered into a ship, and passed over, and came into his own city. ²And, behold, they brought to him a man sick of the palsy, lying on a bed: and Jesus seeing their faith said unto the sick of the palsy, 'Son, be of good cheer; thy sins be forgiven thee.' ³And, behold, certain of the scribes said within themselves, 'This man blasphemeth.' ⁴And Jesus knowing their thoughts said, 'Wherefore think ye evil in your hearts? ⁵For whether is easier, to say, "Thy sins be forgiven thee," or to say, "Arise, and walk"? ⁶But that ye may know that the Son of man hath power on earth to forgive sins,' then saith he to the sick of the palsy, 'Arise, take up thy bed, and go unto thine house.' ⁷And he arose, and departed to his house. ⁸But when the multitudes saw it, they marvelled, and glorified God, which had given such power unto men.

⁹And as Jesus passed forth from thence, he saw a man, named Matthew, sitting at the receipt of custom, and he saith unto him, 'Follow me.' And he arose, and followed him.

¹⁰And it came to pass, as Jesus sat at meat in the house, behold, many publicans and sinners came and sat down with him and his disciples. ¹¹And when the Pharisees saw it, they said unto his disciples, 'Why eateth your Master with publicans and sinners?' ¹²But when Jesus heard that, he said unto them, 'They that be whole need not a physician, but they that are sick. ¹³But go ye and learn what that meaneth, "I will have mercy, and not sacrifice," for I am not come to

call the righteous, but sinners to repentance.'

¹⁴ Then came to him the disciples of John, saying, 'Why do we and the Pharisees fast oft, but thy disciples fast not?' ¹⁵And Jesus said unto them, 'Can the children of the bride-chamber mourn, as long as the bridegroom is with them? But the days will come, when the bridegroom shall be taken from them, and then shall they fast. ¹⁶ No man putteth a piece of new cloth unto an old garment, for that which is put in to fill it up taketh from the garment, and the rent is made worse. ¹⁷ Neither do men put new wine into old bottles: else the bottles break, and the wine runneth out, and the bottles perish; but they put new wine into new bottles, and both are preserved.'

¹⁸ While he spake these things unto them, behold, there came a certain ruler, and worshipped him, saying, 'My daughter is even now dead, but come and lay thy hand upon her, and she shall live.' ¹⁹And Jesus arose, and followed him, and so did his disciples.

²⁰And, behold, a woman, which was diseased with an issue of blood twelve years, came behind him, and touched the hem of his garment, ²¹ for she said within herself, 'If I may but touch his garment, I shall be whole.' ²² But Jesus turned him about, and when he saw her, he said, 'Daughter, be of good comfort; thy faith hath made thee whole.' And the woman was made whole from that hour. ²³And when Jesus came into the ruler's house, and saw the minstrels and the people making a noise, ²⁴ he said unto them, 'Give place, for the maid is not dead, but sleepeth.' And they laughed him to scorn. ²⁵ But when the people were put forth, he went in, and took her by the hand, and the maid arose. ²⁶And the fame

hereof went abroad into all that land.

²⁷And when Jesus departed thence, two blind men followed him, crying, and saying, 'Thou Son of David, have mercy on us.' ²⁸And when he was come into the house, the blind men came to him, and Jesus saith unto them, 'Believe ye that I am able to do this?' They said unto him, 'Yea, Lord.' ²⁹Then touched he their eyes, saying, 'According to your faith be it unto you.' ³⁰And their eyes were opened; and Jesus straitly charged them, saying, 'See that no man know it.' ³¹But they, when they were departed, spread abroad his fame in all that country.

³²As they went out, behold, they brought to him a dumb man possessed with a devil. ³³And when the devil was cast out, the dumb spake, and the multitudes marvelled, saying, 'It was never so seen in Israel.' ³⁴But the Pharisees said, 'He casteth out devils through the prince of the devils.' ³⁵And Jesus went about all the cities and villages, teaching in their synagogues, and preaching the gospel of the kingdom, and healing every sickness and every disease among the people.

³⁶But when he saw the multitudes, he was moved with compassion on them, because they fainted, and were scattered abroad, as sheep having no shepherd. ³⁷Then saith he unto his disciples, 'The harvest truly is plenteous, but the labourers are few; ³⁸pray ye therefore the Lord of the harvest, that he will send forth labourers into his harvest.'

10 And when he had called unto him his twelve disciples, he gave them power against unclean spirits, to cast them out, and to heal all manner of sickness and all manner

of disease. ² Now the names of the twelve apostles are these: the first, Simon, who is called Peter, and Andrew his brother; James the son of Zebedee, and John his brother; ³ Philip, and Bartholomew; Thomas, and Matthew the publican; James the son of Alphæus, and Lebbæus, whose surname was Thaddæus; ⁴ Simon the Canaanite, and Judas Iscariot, who also betrayed him. ⁵ These twelve Jesus sent forth, and commanded them, saying, 'Go not into the way of the Gentiles, and into any city of the Samaritans enter ye not: ⁶ but go rather to the lost sheep of the house of Israel. ⁷ And as ye go, preach, saying, "The kingdom of heaven is at hand." ⁸ Heal the sick, cleanse the lepers, raise the dead, cast out devils: freely ye have received, freely give. ⁹ Provide neither gold, nor silver, nor brass in your purses, ¹⁰ nor scrip for your journey, neither two coats, neither shoes, nor yet staves, for the workman is worthy of his meat. ¹¹ And into whatsoever city or town ye shall enter, enquire who in it is worthy; and there abide till ye go thence. ¹² And when ye come into an house, salute it. ¹³ And if the house be worthy, let your peace come upon it: but if it be not worthy, let your peace return to you. ¹⁴ And whosoever shall not receive you, nor hear your words, when ye depart out of that house or city, shake off the dust of your feet. ¹⁵ Verily I say unto you, it shall be more tolerable for the land of Sodom and Gomorrha in the day of judgment, than for that city.

¹⁶ 'Behold, I send you forth as sheep in the midst of wolves: be ye therefore wise as serpents, and harmless as doves. ¹⁷ But beware of men, for they will deliver you up to the councils, and they will scourge you in their synagogues; ¹⁸ and ye shall

be brought before governors and kings for my sake, for a testimony against them and the Gentiles. ¹⁹But when they deliver you up, take no thought how or what ye shall speak, for it shall be given you in that same hour what ye shall speak. ²⁰For it is not ye that speak, but the Spirit of your Father which speaketh in you. ²¹And the brother shall deliver up the brother to death, and the father the child, and the children shall rise up against their parents, and cause them to be put to death. ²²And ye shall be hated of all men for my name's sake: but he that endureth to the end shall be saved. ²³But when they persecute you in this city, flee ye into another, for verily I say unto you, ye shall not have gone over the cities of Israel, till the Son of man be come. ²⁴The disciple is not above his master, nor the servant above his lord. ²⁵It is enough for the disciple that he be as his master, and the servant as his lord. If they have called the master of the house Beelzebub, how much more shall they call them of his household? ²⁶Fear them not therefore, for there is nothing covered, that shall not be revealed; and hid, that shall not be known. ²⁷What I tell you in darkness, that speak ye in light: and what ye hear in the ear, that preach ye upon the housetops. ²⁸And fear not them which kill the body, but are not able to kill the soul, but rather fear him which is able to destroy both soul and body in hell. ²⁹Are not two sparrows sold for a farthing? And one of them shall not fall on the ground without your Father. ³⁰But the very hairs of your head are all numbered. ³¹Fear ye not therefore, ye are of more value than many sparrows. ³²Whosoever therefore shall confess me before men, him will I confess also before my Father which is in heaven.

[33] But whosoever shall deny me before men, him will I also deny before my Father which is in heaven. [34] Think not that I am come to send peace on earth; I came not to send peace, but a sword. [35] For I am come to set a man at variance against his father, and the daughter against her mother, and the daughter-in-law against her mother-in-law. [36] And a man's foes shall be they of his own household. [37] He that loveth father or mother more than me is not worthy of me: and he that loveth son or daughter more than me is not worthy of me. [38] And he that taketh not his cross, and followeth after me, is not worthy of me. [39] He that findeth his life shall lose it: and he that loseth his life for my sake shall find it.

[40] 'He that receiveth you receiveth me, and he that receiveth me receiveth him that sent me. [41] He that receiveth a prophet in the name of a prophet shall receive a prophet's reward; and he that receiveth a righteous man in the name of a righteous man shall receive a righteous man's reward. [42] And whosoever shall give to drink unto one of these little ones a cup of cold water only in the name of a disciple, verily I say unto you, he shall in no wise lose his reward.'

11 And it came to pass, when Jesus had made an end of commanding his twelve disciples, he departed thence to teach and to preach in their cities. [2] Now when John had heard in the prison the works of Christ, he sent two of his disciples, [3] and said unto him, 'Art thou he that should come, or do we look for another?' [4] Jesus answered and said unto them, 'Go and shew John again those things which ye do hear and see: [5] the blind receive their sight, and the lame walk, the lepers are cleansed, and the deaf hear, the dead are raised up, and the poor have the gospel preached to them. ⁶And blessed is he, whosoever shall not be offended in me.'

⁷And as they departed, Jesus began to say unto the multitudes concerning John, 'What went ye out into the wilderness to see? A reed shaken with the wind? ⁸But what went ye out for to see? A man clothed in soft raiment? Behold, they that wear soft clothing are in kings' houses. ⁹But what went ye out for to see? A prophet? Yea, I say unto you, and more than a prophet. ¹⁰For this is he, of whom it is written, "Behold, I send my messenger before thy face, which shall prepare thy way before thee." ¹¹Verily I say unto you, among them that are born of women there hath not risen a greater than John the Baptist; notwithstanding he that is least in the kingdom of heaven is greater than he. ¹²And from the days of John the Baptist until now the kingdom of heaven suffereth violence, and the violent take it by force. ¹³For all the prophets and the law prophesied until John. ¹⁴And if ye will receive it, this is Elias, which was for to come. ¹⁵He that hath ears to hear, let him hear.

¹⁶'But whereunto shall I liken this generation? It is like unto children sitting in the markets, and calling unto their fellows, ¹⁷and saying, "We have piped unto you, and ye have not danced; we have mourned unto you, and ye have not lamented." ¹⁸For John came neither eating nor drinking, and they say, "He hath a devil." ¹⁹The Son of man came eating and drinking, and they say, "Behold a man gluttonous, and a winebibber, a friend of publicans and sinners." But wisdom is justified of her children.'

²⁰ Then began he to upbraid the cities wherein most of his mighty works were done, because they repented not. ²¹ 'Woe unto thee, Chorazin! Woe unto thee, Bethsaida! For if the mighty works, which were done in you, had been done in Tyre and Sidon, they would have repented long ago in sackcloth and ashes. ²² But I say unto you, it shall be more tolerable for Tyre and Sidon at the day of judgment, than for you. ²³ And thou, Capernaum, which art exalted unto heaven, shalt be brought down to hell: for if the mighty works, which have been done in thee, had been done in Sodom, it would have remained until this day. ²⁴ But I say unto you, that it shall be more tolerable for the land of Sodom in the day of judgment, than for thee.'

²⁵ At that time Jesus answered and said, 'I thank thee, O Father, Lord of heaven and earth, because thou hast hid these things from the wise and prudent, and hast revealed them unto babes. ²⁶ Even so, Father, for so it seemed good in thy sight. ²⁷ All things are delivered unto me of my Father, and no man knoweth the Son, but the Father; neither knoweth any man the Father, save the Son, and he to whomsoever the Son will reveal him.

²⁸ 'Come unto me, all ye that labour and are heavy laden, and I will give you rest. ²⁹ Take my yoke upon you, and learn of me; for I am meek and lowly in heart: and ye shall find rest unto your souls. ³⁰ For my yoke is easy, and my burden is light.'

12 At that time Jesus went on the sabbath day through the corn; and his disciples were an hungred, and began to pluck the ears of corn, and to eat. ² But when the Pharisees

saw it, they said unto him, 'Behold, thy disciples do that which is not lawful to do upon the sabbath day.' ³But he said unto them, 'Have ye not read what David did, when he was an hungred, and they that were with him; ⁴how he entered into the house of God, and did eat the shewbread, which was not lawful for him to eat, neither for them which were with him, but only for the priests? ⁵Or have ye not read in the law, how that on the sabbath days the priests in the temple profane the sabbath, and are blameless? ⁶But I say unto you that in this place is one greater than the temple. ⁷But if ye had known what this meaneth, I will have mercy, and not sacrifice, ye would not have condemned the guiltless. ⁸For the Son of man is Lord even of the sabbath day.' ⁹And when he was departed thence, he went into their synagogue.

¹⁰And, behold, there was a man which had his hand withered. And they asked him, saying, 'Is it lawful to heal on the sabbath days?' that they might accuse him. ¹¹And he said unto them, 'What man shall there be among you, that shall have one sheep, and if it fall into a pit on the sabbath day, will he not lay hold on it, and lift it out? ¹²How much then is a man better than a sheep? Wherefore it is lawful to do well on the sabbath days.' ¹³Then saith he to the man, 'Stretch forth thine hand.' And he stretched it forth; and it was restored whole, like as the other.

¹⁴Then the Pharisees went out, and held a council against him, how they might destroy him. ¹⁵But when Jesus knew it, he withdrew himself from thence, and great multitudes followed him, and he healed them all; ¹⁶and charged them that they should not make him known, ¹⁷that it might be fulfilled

which was spoken by Esaias the prophet, saying, ¹⁸ 'Behold my servant, whom I have chosen; my beloved, in whom my soul is well pleased: I will put my spirit upon him, and he shall shew judgment to the Gentiles. ¹⁹ He shall not strive, nor cry; neither shall any man hear his voice in the streets. ²⁰ A bruised reed shall he not break, and smoking flax shall he not quench, till he send forth judgment unto victory. ²¹ And in his name shall the Gentiles trust.'

²² Then was brought unto him one possessed with a devil, blind, and dumb: and he healed him, insomuch that the blind and dumb both spake and saw. ²³ And all the people were amazed, and said, 'Is not this the son of David?' ²⁴ But when the Pharisees heard it, they said, 'This fellow doth not cast out devils, but by Beelzebub the prince of the devils.' ²⁵ And Jesus knew their thoughts, and said unto them, 'Every kingdom divided against itself is brought to desolation; and every city or house divided against itself shall not stand. ²⁶ And if Satan cast out Satan, he is divided against himself; how shall then his kingdom stand? ²⁷ And if I by Beelzebub cast out devils, by whom do your children cast them out? Therefore they shall be your judges. ²⁸ But if I cast out devils by the Spirit of God, then the kingdom of God is come unto you. ²⁹ Or else how can one enter into a strong man's house, and spoil his goods, except he first bind the strong man? And then he will spoil his house. ³⁰ He that is not with me is against me; and he that gathereth not with me scattereth abroad.

³¹ 'Wherefore I say unto you, all manner of sin and blasphemy shall be forgiven unto men: but the blasphemy against the Holy Ghost shall not be forgiven unto men. ³² And who-

soever speaketh a word against the Son of man, it shall be forgiven him: but whosoever speaketh against the Holy Ghost, it shall not be forgiven him, neither in this world, neither in the world to come. ³³ Either make the tree good, and his fruit good, or else make the tree corrupt, and his fruit corrupt: for the tree is known by his fruit. ³⁴ O generation of vipers, how can ye, being evil, speak good things? For out of the abundance of the heart the mouth speaketh. ³⁵ A good man out of the good treasure of the heart bringeth forth good things: and an evil man out of the evil treasure bringeth forth evil things. ³⁶ But I say unto you that every idle word that men shall speak, they shall give account thereof in the day of judgment. ³⁷ For by thy words thou shalt be justified, and by thy words thou shalt be condemned.'

³⁸ Then certain of the scribes and of the Pharisees answered, saying, 'Master, we would see a sign from thee.' ³⁹ But he answered and said unto them, 'An evil and adulterous generation seeketh after a sign; and there shall no sign be given to it, but the sign of the prophet Jonas: ⁴⁰ for as Jonas was three days and three nights in the whale's belly; so shall the Son of man be three days and three nights in the heart of the earth. ⁴¹ The men of Nineveh shall rise in judgment with this generation, and shall condemn it: because they repented at the preaching of Jonas; and, behold, a greater than Jonas is here. ⁴² The queen of the south shall rise up in the judgment with this generation, and shall condemn it: for she came from the uttermost parts of the earth to hear the wisdom of Solomon; and, behold, a greater than Solomon is here. ⁴³ When the unclean spirit is gone out of a man, he walketh through

dry places, seeking rest, and findeth none. ⁴⁴ Then he saith, "I will return into my house from whence I came out"; and when he is come, he findeth it empty, swept, and garnished. ⁴⁵ Then goeth he, and taketh with himself seven other spirits more wicked than himself, and they enter in and dwell there, and the last state of that man is worse than the first. Even so shall it be also unto this wicked generation.'

⁴⁶ While he yet talked to the people, behold, his mother and his brethren stood without, desiring to speak with him. ⁴⁷ Then one said unto him, 'Behold, thy mother and thy brethren stand without, desiring to speak with thee.' ⁴⁸ But he answered and said unto him that told him, 'Who is my mother? And who are my brethren?' ⁴⁹ And he stretched forth his hand toward his disciples, and said, 'Behold my mother and my brethren! ⁵⁰ For whosoever shall do the will of my Father which is in heaven, the same is my brother, and sister, and mother.'

13 The same day went Jesus out of the house, and sat by the sea side. ²And great multitudes were gathered together unto him, so that he went into a ship, and sat; and the whole multitude stood on the shore. ³And he spake many things unto them in parables, saying, 'Behold, a sower went forth to sow; ⁴and when he sowed, some seeds fell by the way side, and the fowls came and devoured them up. ⁵Some fell upon stony places, where they had not much earth: and forthwith they sprung up, because they had no deepness of earth. ⁶And when the sun was up, they were scorched; and because they had no root, they withered away.

⁷And some fell among thorns; and the thorns sprung up, and choked them. ⁸ But other fell into good ground, and brought forth fruit, some an hundredfold, some sixtyfold, some thirty-fold. ⁹ Who hath ears to hear, let him hear.' ¹⁰And the disciples came, and said unto him, 'Why speakest thou unto them in parables?' ¹¹He answered and said unto them, 'Because it is given unto you to know the mysteries of the kingdom of heaven, but to them it is not given. ¹²For whosoever hath, to him shall be given, and he shall have more abundance: but whosoever hath not, from him shall be taken away even that he hath. ¹³Therefore speak I to them in parables: because they seeing see not; and hearing they hear not, neither do they understand. ¹⁴And in them is fulfilled the prophecy of Esaias, which saith, "By hearing ye shall hear, and shall not understand; and seeing ye shall see, and shall not perceive: ¹⁵for this people's heart is waxed gross, and their ears are dull of hearing, and their eyes they have closed, lest at any time they should see with their eyes, and hear with their ears, and should understand with their heart, and should be converted, and I should heal them." ¹⁶But blessed are your eyes, for they see, and your ears, for they hear. ¹⁷For verily I say unto you that many prophets and righteous men have desired to see those things which ye see, and have not seen them; and to hear those things which ye hear, and have not heard them.

¹⁸ 'Hear ye therefore the parable of the sower. ¹⁹When any one heareth the word of the kingdom, and understandeth it not, then cometh the wicked one, and catcheth away that which was sown in his heart. This is he which received seed by the way side. ²⁰But he that received the seed into stony

places, the same is he that heareth the word, and anon with joy receiveth it; ²¹ yet hath he not root in himself, but dureth for a while: for when tribulation or persecution ariseth because of the word, by and by he is offended. ²² He also that received seed among the thorns is he that heareth the word; and the care of this world, and the deceitfulness of riches, choke the word, and he becometh unfruitful. ²³ But he that received seed into the good ground is he that heareth the word, and understandeth it; which also beareth fruit, and bringeth forth, some an hundredfold, some sixty, some thirty.'

²⁴Another parable put he forth unto them, saying, 'The kingdom of heaven is likened unto a man which sowed good seed in his field: ²⁵ but while men slept, his enemy came and sowed tares among the wheat, and went his way. ²⁶ But when the blade was sprung up, and brought forth fruit, then appeared the tares also. ²⁷ So the servants of the householder came and said unto him, "Sir, didst not thou sow good seed in thy field? From whence then hath it tares?" ²⁸ He said unto them, "An enemy hath done this." The servants said unto him, "Wilt thou then that we go and gather them up?" ²⁹ But he said, "Nay, lest while ye gather up the tares, ye root up also the wheat with them. ³⁰ Let both grow together until the harvest: and in the time of harvest I will say to the reapers, 'Gather ye together first the tares, and bind them in bundles to burn them, but gather the wheat into my barn.'"'

³¹Another parable put he forth unto them, saying, 'The kingdom of heaven is like to a grain of mustard seed, which a man took, and sowed in his field, ³² which indeed is the least of all seeds: but when it is grown, it is the greatest among

herbs, and becometh a tree, so that the birds of the air come and lodge in the branches thereof.'

³³Another parable spake he unto them. 'The kingdom of heaven is like unto leaven, which a woman took, and hid in three measures of meal, till the whole was leavened.' ³⁴All these things spake Jesus unto the multitude in parables; and without a parable spake he not unto them, ³⁵ that it might be fulfilled which was spoken by the prophet, saying, 'I will open my mouth in parables; I will utter things which have been kept secret from the foundation of the world.' ³⁶Then Jesus sent the multitude away, and went into the house, and his disciples came unto him, saying, 'Declare unto us the parable of the tares of the field.' ³⁷He answered and said unto them, 'He that soweth the good seed is the Son of man; ³⁸ the field is the world; the good seed are the children of the kingdom; but the tares are the children of the wicked one; ³⁹ the enemy that sowed them is the devil; the harvest is the end of the world; and the reapers are the angels. ⁴⁰As therefore the tares are gathered and burned in the fire, so shall it be in the end of this world. ⁴¹The Son of man shall send forth his angels, and they shall gather out of his kingdom all things that offend, and them which do iniquity, ⁴² and shall cast them into a furnace of fire: there shall be wailing and gnashing of teeth. ⁴³Then shall the righteous shine forth as the sun in the kingdom of their Father. Who hath ears to hear, let him hear.

⁴⁴ 'Again, the kingdom of heaven is like unto treasure hid in a field; the which when a man hath found, he hideth, and for joy thereof goeth and selleth all that he hath, and buyeth that field.

⁴⁵ 'Again, the kingdom of heaven is like unto a merchant man, seeking goodly pearls, ⁴⁶ who, when he had found one pearl of great price, went and sold all that he had, and bought it.

⁴⁷ 'Again, the kingdom of heaven is like unto a net, that was cast into the sea, and gathered of every kind: ⁴⁸ which, when it was full, they drew to shore, and sat down, and gathered the good into vessels, but cast the bad away. ⁴⁹ So shall it be at the end of the world. The angels shall come forth, and sever the wicked from among the just, ⁵⁰ and shall cast them into the furnace of fire: there shall be wailing and gnashing of teeth.' ⁵¹ Jesus saith unto them, 'Have ye understood all these things?' They say unto him, 'Yea, Lord.' ⁵² Then said he unto them, 'Therefore every scribe which is instructed unto the kingdom of heaven is like unto a man that is an householder, which bringeth forth out of his treasure things new and old.'

⁵³ And it came to pass, that when Jesus had finished these parables, he departed thence. ⁵⁴ And when he was come into his own country, he taught them in their synagogue, insomuch that they were astonished, and said, 'Whence hath this man this wisdom, and these mighty works? ⁵⁵ Is not this the carpenter's son? Is not his mother called Mary? And his brethren, James, and Joses, and Simon, and Judas? ⁵⁶ And his sisters, are they not all with us? Whence then hath this man all these things?' ⁵⁷ And they were offended in him. But Jesus said unto them, 'A prophet is not without honour, save in his own country, and in his own house.' ⁵⁸ And he did not many mighty works there because of their unbelief.

14 At that time Herod the tetrarch heard of the fame of Jesus, ²and said unto his servants, 'This is John the Baptist; he is risen from the dead; and therefore mighty works do shew forth themselves in him.'

³For Herod had laid hold on John, and bound him, and put him in prison for Herodias' sake, his brother Philip's wife. ⁴For John said unto him, 'It is not lawful for thee to have her.' ⁵And when he would have put him to death, he feared the multitude, because they counted him as a prophet. ⁶But when Herod's birthday was kept, the daughter of Herodias danced before them, and pleased Herod. ⁷Whereupon he promised with an oath to give her whatsoever she would ask. ⁸And she, being before instructed of her mother, said, 'Give me here John Baptist's head in a charger.' ⁹And the king was sorry; nevertheless for the oath's sake, and them which sat with him at meat, he commanded it to be given her. ¹⁰And he sent, and beheaded John in the prison. ¹¹And his head was brought in a charger, and given to the damsel, and she brought it to her mother. ¹²And his disciples came, and took up the body, and buried it, and went and told Jesus.

¹³When Jesus heard of it, he departed thence by ship into a desert place apart, and when the people had heard thereof, they followed him on foot out of the cities. ¹⁴And Jesus went forth, and saw a great multitude, and was moved with compassion toward them, and he healed their sick.

¹⁵And when it was evening, his disciples came to him, saying, 'This is a desert place, and the time is now past; send the multitude away, that they may go into the villages, and buy themselves victuals.' ¹⁶But Jesus said unto them, 'They

need not depart; give ye them to eat.' ¹⁷And they say unto him, 'We have here but five loaves, and two fishes.' ¹⁸He said, 'Bring them hither to me.' ¹⁹And he commanded the multitude to sit down on the grass, and took the five loaves, and the two fishes, and looking up to heaven, he blessed, and brake, and gave the loaves to his disciples, and the disciples to the multitude. ²⁰And they did all eat, and were filled: and they took up of the fragments that remained twelve baskets full. ²¹And they that had eaten were about five thousand men, beside women and children.

²²And straightway Jesus constrained his disciples to get into a ship, and to go before him unto the other side, while he sent the multitudes away. ²³And when he had sent the multitudes away, he went up into a mountain apart to pray: and when the evening was come, he was there alone. ²⁴But the ship was now in the midst of the sea, tossed with waves: for the wind was contrary. ²⁵And in the fourth watch of the night Jesus went unto them, walking on the sea. ²⁶And when the disciples saw him walking on the sea, they were troubled, saying, 'It is a spirit' and they cried out for fear. ²⁷But straightway Jesus spake unto them, saying, 'Be of good cheer; it is I; be not afraid.' ²⁸And Peter answered him and said, 'Lord, if it be thou, bid me come unto thee on the water.' ²⁹And he said, 'Come.' And when Peter was come down out of the ship, he walked on the water, to go to Jesus. ³⁰But when he saw the wind boisterous, he was afraid; and beginning to sink, he cried, saying, 'Lord, save me.' ³¹And immediately Jesus stretched forth his hand, and caught him, and said unto him, 'O thou of little faith, wherefore didst thou doubt?' ³²And when

they were come into the ship, the wind ceased. ³³ Then they that were in the ship came and worshipped him, saying, 'Of a truth thou art the Son of God.'

³⁴And when they were gone over, they came into the land of Gennesaret. ³⁵And when the men of that place had knowledge of him, they sent out into all that country round about, and brought unto him all that were diseased; ³⁶ and besought him that they might only touch the hem of his garment: and as many as touched were made perfectly whole.

15 Then came to Jesus scribes and Pharisees, which were of Jerusalem, saying, ²'Why do thy disciples transgress the tradition of the elders? For they wash not their hands when they eat bread.' ³But he answered and said unto them, 'Why do ye also transgress the commandment of God by your tradition? ⁴For God commanded, saying, "Honour thy father and mother," and, "He that curseth father or mother, let him die the death." ⁵But ye say, "Whosoever shall say to his father or his mother, 'It is a gift, by whatsoever thou mightest be profited by me' ⁶and honour not his father or his mother, he shall be free." Thus have ye made the commandment of God of none effect by your tradition. ⁷Ye hypocrites, well did Esaias prophesy of you, saying, ⁸ "This people draweth nigh unto me with their mouth, and honoureth me with their lips; but their heart is far from me. ⁹But in vain they do worship me, teaching for doctrines the commandments of men."'

¹⁰And he called the multitude, and said unto them, 'Hear, and understand: ¹¹not that which goeth into the mouth defileth a man; but that which cometh out of the mouth, this

defileth a man.' ¹² Then came his disciples, and said unto him, 'Knowest thou that the Pharisees were offended, after they heard this saying?' ¹³ But he answered and said, 'Every plant, which my heavenly Father hath not planted, shall be rooted up. ¹⁴ Let them alone: they be blind leaders of the blind. And if the blind lead the blind, both shall fall into the ditch.' ¹⁵ Then answered Peter and said unto him, 'Declare unto us this parable.' ¹⁶ And Jesus said, 'Are ye also yet without understanding? ¹⁷ Do not ye yet understand, that whatsoever entereth in at the mouth goeth into the belly, and is cast out into the draught? ¹⁸ But those things which proceed out of the mouth come forth from the heart; and they defile the man. ¹⁹ For out of the heart proceed evil thoughts, murders, adulteries, fornications, thefts, false witness, blasphemies. ²⁰ These are the things which defile a man: but to eat with unwashen hands defileth not a man.'

²¹ Then Jesus went thence, and departed into the coasts of Tyre and Sidon. ²² And, behold, a woman of Canaan came out of the same coasts, and cried unto him, saying, 'Have mercy on me, O Lord, thou Son of David; my daughter is grievously vexed with a devil.' ²³ But he answered her not a word. And his disciples came and besought him, saying, 'Send her away; for she crieth after us.' ²⁴ But he answered and said, 'I am not sent but unto the lost sheep of the house of Israel.' ²⁵ Then came she and worshipped him, saying, 'Lord, help me.' ²⁶ But he answered and said, 'It is not meet to take the children's bread, and to cast it to dogs.' ²⁷ And she said, 'Truth, Lord, yet the dogs eat of the crumbs which fall from their masters' table.' ²⁸ Then Jesus answered and said unto

her, 'O woman, great is thy faith. Be it unto thee even as thou wilt.' And her daughter was made whole from that very hour. ²⁹And Jesus departed from thence, and came nigh unto the sea of Galilee; and went up into a mountain, and sat down there. ³⁰And great multitudes came unto him, having with them those that were lame, blind, dumb, maimed, and many others, and cast them down at Jesus' feet; and he healed them, ³¹insomuch that the multitude wondered, when they saw the dumb to speak, the maimed to be whole, the lame to walk, and the blind to see, and they glorified the God of Israel.

³²Then Jesus called his disciples unto him, and said, 'I have compassion on the multitude, because they continue with me now three days, and have nothing to eat, and I will not send them away fasting, lest they faint in the way.' ³³And his disciples say unto him, 'Whence should we have so much bread in the wilderness, as to fill so great a multitude?' ³⁴And Jesus saith unto them, 'How many loaves have ye?' And they said, 'Seven, and a few little fishes.' ³⁵And he commanded the multitude to sit down on the ground. ³⁶And he took the seven loaves and the fishes, and gave thanks, and brake them, and gave to his disciples, and the disciples to the multitude. ³⁷And they did all eat, and were filled, and they took up of the broken meat that was left seven baskets full. ³⁸And they that did eat were four thousand men, beside women and children. ³⁹And he sent away the multitude, and took ship, and came into the coasts of Magdala.

16 The Pharisees also with the Sadducees came, and tempting desired him that he would shew them a sign from

heaven. ²He answered and said unto them, 'When it is evening, ye say, "It will be fair weather, for the sky is red." ³And in the morning, "It will be foul weather today, for the sky is red and lowring." O ye hypocrites, ye can discern the face of the sky; but can ye not discern the signs of the times? ⁴A wicked and adulterous generation seeketh after a sign; and there shall no sign be given unto it, but the sign of the prophet Jonas.' And he left them, and departed. ⁵And when his disciples were come to the other side, they had forgotten to take bread.

⁶Then Jesus said unto them, 'Take heed and beware of the leaven of the Pharisees and of the Sadducees.' ⁷And they reasoned among themselves, saying, 'It is because we have taken no bread,' ⁸which when Jesus perceived, he said unto them, 'O ye of little faith, why reason ye among yourselves, because ye have brought no bread? ⁹Do ye not yet understand, neither remember the five loaves of the five thousand, and how many baskets ye took up? ¹⁰Neither the seven loaves of the four thousand, and how many baskets ye took up? ¹¹How is it that ye do not understand that I spake it not to you concerning bread, that ye should beware of the leaven of the Pharisees and of the Sadducees?' ¹²Then understood they how that he bade them not beware of the leaven of bread, but of the doctrine of the Pharisees and of the Sadducees.

¹³When Jesus came into the coasts of Cæsarea Philippi, he asked his disciples, saying, 'Whom do men say that I the Son of man am?' ¹⁴And they said, 'Some say that thou art John the Baptist: some, Elias; and others, Jeremias, or one of the prophets.' ¹⁵He saith unto them, 'But whom say ye that I

am?' ¹⁶And Simon Peter answered and said, 'Thou art the Christ, the Son of the living God.' ¹⁷And Jesus answered and said unto him, 'Blessed art thou, Simon Bar-jona, for flesh and blood hath not revealed it unto thee, but my Father which is in heaven. ¹⁸And I say also unto thee that thou art Peter, and upon this rock I will build my church; and the gates of hell shall not prevail against it. ¹⁹And I will give unto thee the keys of the kingdom of heaven, and whatsoever thou shalt bind on earth shall be bound in heaven, and whatsoever thou shalt loose on earth shall be loosed in heaven.' ²⁰Then charged he his disciples that they should tell no man that he was Jesus the Christ.

²¹From that time forth began Jesus to shew unto his disciples, how that he must go unto Jerusalem, and suffer many things of the elders and chief priests and scribes, and be killed, and be raised again the third day. ²²Then Peter took him, and began to rebuke him, saying, 'Be it far from thee, Lord: this shall not be unto thee.' ²³But he turned, and said unto Peter, 'Get thee behind me, Satan. Thou art an offence unto me, for thou savourest not the things that be of God, but those that be of men.'

²⁴Then said Jesus unto his disciples, 'If any man will come after me, let him deny himself, and take up his cross, and follow me. ²⁵For whosoever will save his life shall lose it, and whosoever will lose his life for my sake shall find it. ²⁶For what is a man profited, if he shall gain the whole world, and lose his own soul? Or what shall a man give in exchange for his soul? ²⁷For the Son of man shall come in the glory of his Father with his angels; and then he shall reward every

man according to his works. ²⁸ Verily I say unto you, there be some standing here, which shall not taste of death, till they see the Son of man coming in his kingdom.'

17 And after six days Jesus taketh Peter, James, and John his brother, and bringeth them up into an high mountain apart, ²and was transfigured before them, and his face did shine as the sun, and his raiment was white as the light. ³And, behold, there appeared unto them Moses and Elias talking with him. ⁴Then answered Peter, and said unto Jesus, 'Lord, it is good for us to be here: if thou wilt, let us make here three tabernacles; one for thee, and one for Moses, and one for Elias.' ⁵While he yet spake, behold, a bright cloud overshadowed them, and behold a voice out of the cloud, which said, 'This is my beloved Son, in whom I am well pleased; hear ye him.' ⁶And when the disciples heard it, they fell on their face, and were sore afraid. ⁷And Jesus came and touched them, and said, 'Arise, and be not afraid.' ⁸And when they had lifted up their eyes, they saw no man, save Jesus only. ⁹And as they came down from the mountain, Jesus charged them, saying, 'Tell the vision to no man, until the Son of man be risen again from the dead.' ¹⁰And his disciples asked him, saying, 'Why then say the scribes that Elias must first come?' ¹¹And Jesus answered and said unto them, 'Elias truly shall first come, and restore all things. ¹²But I say unto you that Elias is come already, and they knew him not, but have done unto him whatsoever they listed. Likewise shall also the Son of man suffer of them.' ¹³Then the disciples understood that he spake unto them of John the Baptist.

¹⁴And when they were come to the multitude, there came to him a certain man, kneeling down to him, and saying, ¹⁵'Lord, have mercy on my son, for he is lunatick, and sore vexed, for ofttimes he falleth into the fire, and oft into the water. ¹⁶And I brought him to thy disciples, and they could not cure him.' ¹⁷Then Jesus answered and said, 'O faithless and perverse generation, how long shall I be with you? How long shall I suffer you? Bring him hither to me.' ¹⁸And Jesus rebuked the devil; and he departed out of him, and the child was cured from that very hour. ¹⁹Then came the disciples to Jesus apart, and said, 'Why could not we cast him out?' ²⁰And Jesus said unto them, 'Because of your unbelief: for verily I say unto you, if ye have faith as a grain of mustard seed, ye shall say unto this mountain, "Remove hence to yonder place," and it shall remove; and nothing shall be impossible unto you. ²¹Howbeit this kind goeth not out but by prayer and fasting.'

²²And while they abode in Galilee, Jesus said unto them, 'The Son of man shall be betrayed into the hands of men: ²³and they shall kill him, and the third day he shall be raised again.' And they were exceeding sorry.

²⁴And when they were come to Capernaum, they that received tribute money came to Peter, and said, 'Doth not your master pay tribute?' ²⁵He saith, 'Yes.' And when he was come into the house, Jesus prevented him, saying, 'What thinkest thou, Simon? Of whom do the kings of the earth take custom or tribute? Of their own children, or of strangers?' ²⁶Peter saith unto him, 'Of strangers.' Jesus saith unto him, 'Then are the children free. ²⁷Notwithstanding, lest we should

offend them, go thou to the sea, and cast an hook, and take up the fish that first cometh up; and when thou hast opened his mouth, thou shalt find a piece of money; that take, and give unto them for me and thee.'

18 At the same time came the disciples unto Jesus, saying, 'Who is the greatest in the kingdom of heaven?' ²And Jesus called a little child unto him, and set him in the midst of them, ³and said, 'Verily I say unto you, except ye be converted, and become as little children, ye shall not enter into the kingdom of heaven. ⁴Whosoever therefore shall humble himself as this little child, the same is greatest in the kingdom of heaven. ⁵And whoso shall receive one such little child in my name receiveth me. ⁶But whoso shall offend one of these little ones which believe in me, it were better for him that a millstone were hanged about his neck, and that he were drowned in the depth of the sea.

⁷'Woe unto the world because of offences! For it must needs be that offences come; but woe to that man by whom the offence cometh! ⁸Wherefore if thy hand or thy foot offend thee, cut them off, and cast them from thee: it is better for thee to enter into life halt or maimed, rather than having two hands or two feet to be cast into everlasting fire. ⁹And if thine eye offend thee, pluck it out, and cast it from thee: it is better for thee to enter into life with one eye, rather than having two eyes to be cast into hell fire. ¹⁰Take heed that ye despise not one of these little ones; for I say unto you, that in heaven their angels do always behold the face of my Father which is in heaven. ¹¹For the Son of man is come to save that

which was lost. ¹² How think ye? If a man have an hundred sheep, and one of them be gone astray, doth he not leave the ninety and nine, and goeth into the mountains, and seeketh that which is gone astray? ¹³ And if so be that he find it, verily I say unto you, he rejoiceth more of that sheep, than of the ninety and nine which went not astray. ¹⁴ Even so it is not the will of your Father which is in heaven, that one of these little ones should perish.

¹⁵ 'Moreover if thy brother shall trespass against thee, go and tell him his fault between thee and him alone: if he shall hear thee, thou hast gained thy brother. ¹⁶ But if he will not hear thee, then take with thee one or two more, that in the mouth of two or three witnesses every word may be established. ¹⁷ And if he shall neglect to hear them, tell it unto the church: but if he neglect to hear the church, let him be unto thee as an heathen man and a publican. ¹⁸ Verily I say unto you, whatsoever ye shall bind on earth shall be bound in heaven, and whatsoever ye shall loose on earth shall be loosed in heaven. ¹⁹ Again I say unto you that if two of you shall agree on earth as touching any thing that they shall ask, it shall be done for them of my Father which is in heaven. ²⁰ For where two or three are gathered together in my name, there am I in the midst of them.'

²¹ Then came Peter to him, and said, 'Lord, how oft shall my brother sin against me, and I forgive him? Till seven times?' ²² Jesus saith unto him, 'I say not unto thee, "Until seven times," but, "Until seventy times seven."

²³ 'Therefore is the kingdom of heaven likened unto a certain king, which would take account of his servants. ²⁴ And

when he had begun to reckon, one was brought unto him, which owed him ten thousand talents. ²⁵ But forasmuch as he had not to pay, his lord commanded him to be sold, and his wife, and children, and all that he had, and payment to be made. ²⁶ The servant therefore fell down, and worshipped him, saying, "Lord, have patience with me, and I will pay thee all." ²⁷ Then the lord of that servant was moved with compassion, and loosed him, and forgave him the debt. ²⁸ But the same servant went out, and found one of his fellowservants, which owed him an hundred pence, and he laid hands on him, and took him by the throat, saying, "Pay me that thou owest." ²⁹ And his fellowservant fell down at his feet, and besought him, saying, "Have patience with me, and I will pay thee all." ³⁰ And he would not, but went and cast him into prison, till he should pay the debt. ³¹ So when his fellowservants saw what was done, they were very sorry, and came and told unto their lord all that was done. ³² Then his lord, after that he had called him, said unto him, "O thou wicked servant, I forgave thee all that debt, because thou desiredst me. ³³ Shouldest not thou also have had compassion on thy fellowservant, even as I had pity on thee?" ³⁴ And his lord was wroth, and delivered him to the tormentors, till he should pay all that was due unto him. ³⁵ So likewise shall my heavenly Father do also unto you, if ye from your hearts forgive not every one his brother their trespasses.'

19 And it came to pass, that when Jesus had finished these sayings, he departed from Galilee, and came into the coasts of Judæa beyond Jordan; ²and great multitudes

followed him; and he healed them there.

³ The Pharisees also came unto him, tempting him, and saying unto him, 'Is it lawful for a man to put away his wife for every cause?' ⁴And he answered and said unto them, 'Have ye not read, that he which made them at the beginning made them male and female, ⁵and said, "For this cause shall a man leave father and mother, and shall cleave to his wife, and they twain shall be one flesh"? ⁶Wherefore they are no more twain, but one flesh. What therefore God hath joined together, let not man put asunder.' ⁷They say unto him, 'Why did Moses then command to give a writing of divorcement, and to put her away?' ⁸He saith unto them, 'Moses, because of the hardness of your hearts suffered you to put away your wives: but from the beginning it was not so. ⁹And I say unto you, whosoever shall put away his wife, except it be for fornication, and shall marry another, committeth adultery: and whoso marrieth her which is put away doth commit adultery.'

¹⁰His disciples say unto him, 'If the case of the man be so with his wife, it is not good to marry.' ¹¹But he said unto them, 'All men cannot receive this saying, save they to whom it is given. ¹²For there are some eunuchs, which were so born from their mother's womb, and there are some eunuchs, which were made eunuchs of men, and there be eunuchs, which have made themselves eunuchs for the kingdom of heaven's sake. He that is able to receive it, let him receive it.'

¹³Then were there brought unto him little children, that he should put his hands on them, and pray, and the disciples rebuked them. ¹⁴But Jesus said, 'Suffer little children, and

forbid them not, to come unto me, for of such is the kingdom of heaven.' ¹⁵And he laid his hands on them, and departed thence.

¹⁶And, behold, one came and said unto him, 'Good Master, what good thing shall I do, that I may have eternal life?' ¹⁷And he said unto him, 'Why callest thou me good? There is none good but one, that is, God: but if thou wilt enter into life, keep the commandments.' ¹⁸He saith unto him, 'Which?' Jesus said, 'Thou shalt do no murder, thou shalt not commit adultery, thou shalt not steal, thou shalt not bear false witness, ¹⁹honour thy father and thy mother, and thou shalt love thy neighbour as thyself.' ²⁰The young man saith unto him, 'All these things have I kept from my youth up; what lack I yet?' ²¹Jesus said unto him, 'If thou wilt be perfect, go and sell that thou hast, and give to the poor, and thou shalt have treasure in heaven, and come and follow me.' ²²But when the young man heard that saying, he went away sorrowful, for he had great possessions.

²³Then said Jesus unto his disciples, 'Verily I say unto you, that a rich man shall hardly enter into the kingdom of heaven. ²⁴And again I say unto you, it is easier for a camel to go through the eye of a needle, than for a rich man to enter into the kingdom of God.' ²⁵When his disciples heard it, they were exceedingly amazed, saying, 'Who then can be saved?' ²⁶But Jesus beheld them, and said unto them, 'With men this is impossible; but with God all things are possible.'

²⁷Then answered Peter and said unto him, 'Behold, we have forsaken all, and followed thee; what shall we have therefore?' ²⁸And Jesus said unto them, 'Verily I say unto you that ye which have followed me, in the regeneration

when the Son of man shall sit in the throne of his glory, ye also shall sit upon twelve thrones, judging the twelve tribes of Israel. ²⁹And every one that hath forsaken houses, or brethren, or sisters, or father, or mother, or wife, or children, or lands, for my name's sake, shall receive an hundredfold, and shall inherit everlasting life. ³⁰But many that are first shall be last; and the last shall be first.

20

¹For the kingdom of heaven is like unto a man that is an householder, which went out early in the morning to hire labourers into his vineyard. ²And when he had agreed with the labourers for a penny a day, he sent them into his vineyard. ³And he went out about the third hour, and saw others standing idle in the marketplace, ⁴and said unto them, "Go ye also into the vineyard, and whatsoever is right I will give you." And they went their way. ⁵Again he went out about the sixth and ninth hour, and did likewise. ⁶And about the eleventh hour he went out, and found others standing idle, and saith unto them, "Why stand ye here all the day idle?" ⁷They say unto him, "Because no man hath hired us." He saith unto them, "Go ye also into the vineyard; and whatsoever is right, that shall ye receive." ⁸So when even was come, the lord of the vineyard saith unto his steward, "Call the labourers, and give them their hire, beginning from the last unto the first." ⁹And when they came that were hired about the eleventh hour, they received every man a penny. ¹⁰But when the first came, they supposed that they should have received more; and they likewise received every man a penny. ¹¹And when they had received it, they

murmured against the goodman of the house, ¹²saying, "These last have wrought but one hour, and thou hast made them equal unto us, which have borne the burden and heat of the day." ¹³But he answered one of them, and said, "Friend, I do thee no wrong; didst not thou agree with me for a penny? ¹⁴Take that thine is, and go thy way: I will give unto this last, even as unto thee. ¹⁵Is it not lawful for me to do what I will with mine own? Is thine eye evil, because I am good?" ¹⁶So the last shall be first, and the first last: for many be called, but few chosen.'

¹⁷And Jesus going up to Jerusalem took the twelve disciples apart in the way, and said unto them, ¹⁸'Behold, we go up to Jerusalem; and the Son of man shall be betrayed unto the chief priests and unto the scribes, and they shall condemn him to death, ¹⁹and shall deliver him to the Gentiles to mock, and to scourge, and to crucify him, and the third day he shall rise again.'

²⁰Then came to him the mother of Zebedee's children with her sons, worshipping him, and desiring a certain thing of him. ²¹And he said unto her, 'What wilt thou?' She saith unto him, 'Grant that these my two sons may sit, the one on thy right hand, and the other on the left, in thy kingdom.' ²²But Jesus answered and said, 'Ye know not what ye ask. Are ye able to drink of the cup that I shall drink of, and to be baptized with the baptism that I am baptized with?' They say unto him, 'We are able.' ²³And he saith unto them, 'Ye shall drink indeed of my cup, and be baptized with the baptism that I am baptized with: but to sit on my right hand, and on my left, is not mine to give, but it shall be given to

them for whom it is prepared of my Father.' ²⁴And when the ten heard it, they were moved with indignation against the two brethren. ²⁵But Jesus called them unto him, and said, 'Ye know that the princes of the Gentiles exercise dominion over them, and they that are great exercise authority upon them. ²⁶But it shall not be so among you: but whosoever will be great among you, let him be your minister; ²⁷and whosoever will be chief among you, let him be your servant. ²⁸Even as the Son of man came not to be ministered unto, but to minister, and to give his life a ransom for many. ²⁹And as they departed from Jericho, a great multitude followed him.

³⁰And, behold, two blind men sitting by the way side, when they heard that Jesus passed by, cried out, saying, 'Have mercy on us, O Lord, thou Son of David.' ³¹And the multitude rebuked them, because they should hold their peace: but they cried the more, saying, 'Have mercy on us, O Lord, thou Son of David.' ³²And Jesus stood still, and called them, and said, 'What will ye that I shall do unto you?' ³³They say unto him, 'Lord, that our eyes may be opened.' ³⁴So Jesus had compassion on them, and touched their eyes, and immediately their eyes received sight, and they followed him.

21 And when they drew nigh unto Jerusalem, and were come to Bethphage, unto the mount of Olives, then sent Jesus two disciples, ²saying unto them, 'Go into the village over against you, and straightway ye shall find an ass tied, and a colt with her; loose them, and bring them unto me. ³And if any man say ought unto you, ye shall say, "The Lord hath need of them," and straightway he will send them.'

⁴All this was done, that it might be fulfilled which was spoken by the prophet, saying, ⁵'Tell ye the daughter of Sion, "Behold, thy King cometh unto thee, meek, and sitting upon an ass, and a colt the foal of an ass."' ⁶And the disciples went, and did as Jesus commanded them, ⁷and brought the ass, and the colt, and put on them their clothes, and they set him thereon. ⁸And a very great multitude spread their garments in the way; others cut down branches from the trees, and strawed them in the way. ⁹And the multitudes that went before, and that followed, cried, saying, 'Hosanna to the Son of David. Blessed is he that cometh in the name of the Lord. Hosanna in the highest.' ¹⁰And when he was come into Jerusalem, all the city was moved, saying, 'Who is this?' ¹¹And the multitude said, 'This is Jesus the prophet of Nazareth of Galilee.'

¹²And Jesus went into the temple of God, and cast out all them that sold and bought in the temple, and overthrew the tables of the moneychangers, and the seats of them that sold doves, ¹³and said unto them, 'It is written, "My house shall be called the house of prayer," but ye have made it a den of thieves.' ¹⁴And the blind and the lame came to him in the temple; and he healed them. ¹⁵And when the chief priests and scribes saw the wonderful things that he did, and the children crying in the temple, and saying, 'Hosanna to the Son of David,' they were sore displeased, ¹⁶and said unto him, 'Hearest thou what these say?' And Jesus saith unto them, 'Yea; have ye never read, "Out of the mouth of babes and sucklings thou hast perfected praise"?'

¹⁷And he left them, and went out of the city into Bethany; and he lodged there. ¹⁸Now in the morning as he returned

into the city, he hungered. ¹⁹And when he saw a fig tree in the way, he came to it, and found nothing thereon, but leaves only, and said unto it, 'Let no fruit grow on thee henceforward for ever.' And presently the fig tree withered away. ²⁰And when the disciples saw it, they marvelled, saying, 'How soon is the fig tree withered away!' ²¹Jesus answered and said unto them, 'Verily I say unto you, if ye have faith, and doubt not, ye shall not only do this which is done to the fig tree, but also if ye shall say unto this mountain, "Be thou removed, and be thou cast into the sea," it shall be done. ²²And all things, whatsoever ye shall ask in prayer, believing, ye shall receive.'

²³And when he was come into the temple, the chief priests and the elders of the people came unto him as he was teaching, and said, 'By what authority doest thou these things? And who gave thee this authority?' ²⁴And Jesus answered and said unto them, 'I also will ask you one thing, which if ye tell me, I in like wise will tell you by what authority I do these things. ²⁵The baptism of John, whence was it? From heaven, or of men?' And they reasoned with themselves, saying, 'If we shall say, "From heaven," he will say unto us, "Why did ye not then believe him?" ²⁶But if we shall say, "Of men," we fear the people, for all hold John as a prophet.' ²⁷And they answered Jesus, and said, 'We cannot tell.' And he said unto them, 'Neither tell I you by what authority I do these things.

²⁸'But what think ye? A certain man had two sons; and he came to the first, and said, "Son, go work to day in my vineyard." ²⁹He answered and said, "I will not," but afterward he

repented, and went. ³⁰And he came to the second, and said likewise. And he answered and said, "I go, sir," and went not. ³¹Whether of them twain did the will of his father?' They say unto him, 'The first.' Jesus saith unto them, 'Verily I say unto you that the publicans and the harlots go into the kingdom of God before you. ³²For John came unto you in the way of righteousness, and ye believed him not: but the publicans and the harlots believed him, and ye, when ye had seen it, repented not afterward, that ye might believe him.

³³'Hear another parable. There was a certain householder, which planted a vineyard, and hedged it round about, and digged a winepress in it, and built a tower, and let it out to husbandmen, and went into a far country. ³⁴And when the time of the fruit drew near, he sent his servants to the husbandmen, that they might receive the fruits of it. ³⁵And the husbandmen took his servants, and beat one, and killed another, and stoned another. ³⁶Again, he sent other servants more than the first, and they did unto them likewise. ³⁷But last of all he sent unto them his son, saying, "They will reverence my son." ³⁸But when the husbandmen saw the son, they said among themselves, "This is the heir; come, let us kill him, and let us seize on his inheritance." ³⁹And they caught him, and cast him out of the vineyard, and slew him. ⁴⁰When the lord therefore of the vineyard cometh, what will he do unto those husbandmen?' ⁴¹They say unto him, 'He will miserably destroy those wicked men, and will let out his vineyard unto other husbandmen, which shall render him the fruits in their seasons.' ⁴²Jesus saith unto them, 'Did ye never read in the scriptures, "The stone which the builders rejected,

the same is become the head of the corner: this is the Lord's doing, and it is marvellous in our eyes"? ⁴³ Therefore say I unto you, the kingdom of God shall be taken from you, and given to a nation bringing forth the fruits thereof. ⁴⁴ And whosoever shall fall on this stone shall be broken, but on whomsoever it shall fall, it will grind him to powder.' ⁴⁵ And when the chief priests and Pharisees had heard his parables, they perceived that he spake of them. ⁴⁶ But when they sought to lay hands on him, they feared the multitude, because they took him for a prophet.

22 And Jesus answered and spake unto them again by parables, and said, ² 'The kingdom of heaven is like unto a certain king, which made a marriage for his son, ³ and sent forth his servants to call them that were bidden to the wedding, and they would not come. ⁴ Again, he sent forth other servants, saying, "Tell them which are bidden, 'Behold, I have prepared my dinner: my oxen and my fatlings are killed, and all things are ready; come unto the marriage.'" ⁵ But they made light of it, and went their ways, one to his farm, another to his merchandise, ⁶ and the remnant took his servants, and entreated them spitefully, and slew them. ⁷ But when the king heard thereof, he was wroth, and he sent forth his armies, and destroyed those murderers, and burned up their city. ⁸ Then saith he to his servants, "The wedding is ready, but they which were bidden were not worthy. ⁹ Go ye therefore into the highways, and as many as ye shall find, bid to the marriage." ¹⁰ So those servants went out into the highways, and gathered together all as many as they found, both

bad and good, and the wedding was furnished with guests.

¹¹ 'And when the king came in to see the guests, he saw there a man which had not on a wedding garment, ¹² and he saith unto him, "Friend, how camest thou in hither not having a wedding garment?" And he was speechless. ¹³ Then said the king to the servants, "Bind him hand and foot, and take him away, and cast him into outer darkness: there shall be weeping and gnashing of teeth." ¹⁴ For many are called, but few are chosen.'

¹⁵ Then went the Pharisees, and took counsel how they might entangle him in his talk. ¹⁶ And they sent out unto him their disciples with the Herodians, saying, 'Master, we know that thou art true, and teachest the way of God in truth, neither carest thou for any man, for thou regardest not the person of men. ¹⁷ Tell us therefore, what thinkest thou? Is it lawful to give tribute unto Caesar, or not?' ¹⁸ But Jesus perceived their wickedness, and said, 'Why tempt ye me, ye hypocrites? ¹⁹ Shew me the tribute money.' And they brought unto him a penny. ²⁰ And he saith unto them, 'Whose is this image and superscription?' ²¹ They say unto him, 'Caesar's.' Then saith he unto them, 'Render therefore unto Caesar the things which are Caesar's; and unto God the things that are God's.' ²² When they had heard these words, they marvelled, and left him, and went their way.

²³ The same day came to him the Sadducees, which say that there is no resurrection, and asked him, ²⁴ saying, 'Master, Moses said, "If a man die, having no children, his brother shall marry his wife, and raise up seed unto his brother." ²⁵ Now there were with us seven brethren, and the first,

when he had married a wife, deceased, and, having no issue, left his wife unto his brother: ²⁶ likewise the second also, and the third, unto the seventh. ²⁷And last of all the woman died also. ²⁸ Therefore in the resurrection whose wife shall she be of the seven? For they all had her.' ²⁹ Jesus answered and said unto them, 'Ye do err, not knowing the scriptures, nor the power of God. ³⁰ For in the resurrection they neither marry, nor are given in marriage, but are as the angels of God in heaven. ³¹ But as touching the resurrection of the dead, have ye not read that which was spoken unto you by God, saying, ³² "I am the God of Abraham, and the God of Isaac, and the God of Jacob?" God is not the God of the dead, but of the living.' ³³And when the multitude heard this, they were astonished at his doctrine.

³⁴ But when the Pharisees had heard that he had put the Sadducees to silence, they were gathered together. ³⁵ Then one of them, which was a lawyer, asked him a question, tempting him, and saying, ³⁶ 'Master, which is the great commandment in the law?' ³⁷ Jesus said unto him, '"Thou shalt love the Lord thy God with all thy heart, and with all thy soul, and with all thy mind." ³⁸ This is the first and great commandment. ³⁹And the second is like unto it, "Thou shalt love thy neighbour as thyself." ⁴⁰ On these two commandments hang all the law and the prophets.'

⁴¹ While the Pharisees were gathered together, Jesus asked them, ⁴² saying, 'What think ye of Christ? Whose son is he?' They say unto him, 'The Son of David.' ⁴³ He saith unto them, 'How then doth David in spirit call him "Lord", saying, ⁴⁴ "The Lord said unto my Lord, 'Sit thou on my right hand,

till I make thine enemies thy footstool'?" ⁴⁵ If David then call him "Lord", how is he his son?' ⁴⁶And no man was able to answer him a word, neither durst any man from that day forth ask him any more questions.

23 Then spake Jesus to the multitude, and to his disciples, ² saying, 'The scribes and the Pharisees sit in Moses' seat; ³ all therefore whatsoever they bid you observe, that observe and do; but do not ye after their works, for they say, and do not. ⁴ For they bind heavy burdens and grievous to be borne, and lay them on men's shoulders; but they themselves will not move them with one of their fingers. ⁵ But all their works they do for to be seen of men; they make broad their phylacteries, and enlarge the borders of their garments, ⁶ and love the uppermost rooms at feasts, and the chief seats in the synagogues, ⁷and greetings in the markets, and to be called of men, "Rabbi, Rabbi". ⁸ But be not ye called Rabbi: for one is your Master, even Christ; and all ye are brethren. ⁹And call no man your father upon the earth: for one is your Father, which is in heaven. ¹⁰Neither be ye called masters: for one is your Master, even Christ. ¹¹ But he that is greatest among you shall be your servant. ¹²And whosoever shall exalt himself shall be abased; and he that shall humble himself shall be exalted.

¹³ 'But woe unto you, scribes and Pharisees, hypocrites! For ye shut up the kingdom of heaven against men, for ye neither go in yourselves, neither suffer ye them that are entering to go in. ¹⁴ Woe unto you, scribes and Pharisees, hypocrites! For ye devour widows' houses, and for a pretence

make long prayer: therefore ye shall receive the greater damnation. [15] Woe unto you, scribes and Pharisees, hypocrites! For ye compass sea and land to make one proselyte, and when he is made, ye make him twofold more the child of hell than yourselves. [16] Woe unto you, ye blind guides, which say, "Whosoever shall swear by the temple, it is nothing; but whosoever shall swear by the gold of the temple, he is a debtor!" [17] Ye fools and blind: for whether is greater, the gold, or the temple that sanctifieth the gold? [18] And, "Whosoever shall swear by the altar, it is nothing; but whosoever sweareth by the gift that is upon it, he is guilty." [19] Ye fools and blind: for whether is greater, the gift, or the altar that sanctifieth the gift? [20] Whoso therefore shall swear by the altar, sweareth by it, and by all things thereon. [21] And whoso shall swear by the temple, sweareth by it, and by him that dwelleth therein. [22] And he that shall swear by heaven, sweareth by the throne of God, and by him that sitteth thereon. [23] Woe unto you, scribes and Pharisees, hypocrites! For ye pay tithe of mint and anise and cummin, and have omitted the weightier matters of the law, judgment, mercy, and faith. These ought ye to have done, and not to leave the other undone. [24] Ye blind guides, which strain at a gnat, and swallow a camel. [25] Woe unto you, scribes and Pharisees, hypocrites! For ye make clean the outside of the cup and of the platter, but within they are full of extortion and excess. [26] Thou blind Pharisee, cleanse first that which is within the cup and platter, that the outside of them may be clean also. [27] Woe unto you, scribes and Pharisees, hypocrites! For ye are like unto whited sepulchres, which indeed appear beautiful outward, but are within full of dead men's bones, and of all uncleanness. ²⁸ Even so ye also outwardly appear righteous unto men, but within ye are full of hypocrisy and iniquity. ²⁹ Woe unto you, scribes and Pharisees, hypocrites! Because ye build the tombs of the prophets, and garnish the sepulchres of the righteous, ³⁰ and say, "If we had been in the days of our fathers, we would not have been partakers with them in the blood of the prophets." ³¹ Wherefore ye be witnesses unto yourselves, that ye are the children of them which killed the prophets. ³² Fill ye up then the measure of your fathers. ³³ Ye serpents, ye generation of vipers, how can ye escape the damnation of hell?

³⁴ 'Wherefore, behold, I send unto you prophets, and wise men, and scribes: and some of them ye shall kill and crucify; and some of them shall ye scourge in your synagogues, and persecute them from city to city: ³⁵ that upon you may come all the righteous blood shed upon the earth, from the blood of righteous Abel unto the blood of Zacharias son of Barachias, whom ye slew between the temple and the altar. ³⁶ Verily I say unto you, all these things shall come upon this generation. ³⁷ O Jerusalem, Jerusalem, thou that killest the prophets, and stonest them which are sent unto thee, how often would I have gathered thy children together, even as a hen gathereth her chickens under her wings, and ye would not! ³⁸ Behold, your house is left unto you desolate. ³⁹ For I say unto you, ye shall not see me henceforth, till ye shall say, "Blessed is he that cometh in the name of the Lord."'

24 And Jesus went out, and departed from the temple, and his disciples came to him for to shew him the

buildings of the temple. ²And Jesus said unto them, 'See ye not all these things? Verily I say unto you, there shall not be left here one stone upon another, that shall not be thrown down.'

³And as he sat upon the mount of Olives, the disciples came unto him privately, saying, 'Tell us, when shall these things be? And what shall be the sign of thy coming, and of the end of the world?' ⁴And Jesus answered and said unto them, 'Take heed that no man deceive you. ⁵For many shall come in my name, saying, "I am Christ," and shall deceive many. ⁶And ye shall hear of wars and rumours of wars; see that ye be not troubled, for all these things must come to pass, but the end is not yet. ⁷For nation shall rise against nation, and kingdom against kingdom, and there shall be famines, and pestilences, and earthquakes, in diverse places. ⁸All these are the beginning of sorrows. ⁹Then shall they deliver you up to be afflicted, and shall kill you, and ye shall be hated of all nations for my name's sake. ¹⁰And then shall many be offended, and shall betray one another, and shall hate one another. ¹¹And many false prophets shall rise, and shall deceive many. ¹²And because iniquity shall abound, the love of many shall wax cold. ¹³But he that shall endure unto the end, the same shall be saved. ¹⁴And this gospel of the kingdom shall be preached in all the world for a witness unto all nations; and then shall the end come. ¹⁵When ye therefore shall see the abomination of desolation, spoken of by Daniel the prophet, stand in the holy place (whoso readeth, let him understand), ¹⁶then let them which be in Judæa flee into the mountains; ¹⁷let him which is on the housetop not come down to take any thing out of his house: ¹⁸neither let him

which is in the field return back to take his clothes. ¹⁹And woe unto them that are with child, and to them that give suck in those days! ²⁰But pray ye that your flight be not in the winter, neither on the sabbath day. ²¹For then shall be great tribulation, such as was not since the beginning of the world to this time, no, nor ever shall be. ²²And except those days should be shortened, there should no flesh be saved, but for the elect's sake those days shall be shortened. ²³Then if any man shall say unto you, "Lo, here is Christ," or "There," believe it not. ²⁴For there shall arise false Christs, and false prophets, and shall shew great signs and wonders; insomuch that, if it were possible, they shall deceive the very elect. ²⁵Behold, I have told you before. ²⁶Wherefore if they shall say unto you, "Behold, he is in the desert," go not forth; "Behold, he is in the secret chambers," believe it not. ²⁷For as the lightning cometh out of the east, and shineth even unto the west; so shall also the coming of the Son of man be. ²⁸For wheresoever the carcase is, there will the eagles be gathered together.

²⁹'Immediately after the tribulation of those days shall the sun be darkened, and the moon shall not give her light, and the stars shall fall from heaven, and the powers of the heavens shall be shaken. ³⁰And then shall appear the sign of the Son of man in heaven, and then shall all the tribes of the earth mourn, and they shall see the Son of man coming in the clouds of heaven with power and great glory. ³¹And he shall send his angels with a great sound of a trumpet, and they shall gather together his elect from the four winds, from one end of heaven to the other. ³²Now learn a parable of the fig tree. When his branch is yet tender, and putteth

forth leaves, ye know that summer is nigh: ³³ so likewise ye, when ye shall see all these things, know that it is near, even at the doors. ³⁴ Verily I say unto you, this generation shall not pass, till all these things be fulfilled. ³⁵ Heaven and earth shall pass away, but my words shall not pass away.

³⁶ 'But of that day and hour knoweth no man, no, not the angels of heaven, but my Father only. ³⁷ But as the days of Noe were, so shall also the coming of the Son of man be. ³⁸ For as in the days that were before the flood they were eating and drinking, marrying and giving in marriage, until the day that Noe entered into the ark, ³⁹ and knew not until the flood came, and took them all away; so shall also the coming of the Son of man be. ⁴⁰ Then shall two be in the field; the one shall be taken, and the other left. ⁴¹ Two women shall be grinding at the mill; the one shall be taken, and the other left.

⁴² 'Watch therefore: for ye know not what hour your Lord doth come. ⁴³ But know this, that if the goodman of the house had known in what watch the thief would come, he would have watched, and would not have suffered his house to be broken up. ⁴⁴ Therefore be ye also ready: for in such an hour as ye think not the Son of man cometh. ⁴⁵ Who then is a faithful and wise servant, whom his lord hath made ruler over his household, to give them meat in due season? ⁴⁶ Blessed is that servant, whom his lord when he cometh shall find so doing. ⁴⁷ Verily I say unto you that he shall make him ruler over all his goods. ⁴⁸ But and if that evil servant shall say in his heart, "My lord delayeth his coming," ⁴⁹ and shall begin to smite his fellow-servants, and to eat and drink with the drunken; ⁵⁰ the lord of that servant shall come in a day when

he looketh not for him, and in an hour that he is not aware of, ⁵¹and shall cut him asunder, and appoint him his portion with the hypocrites: there shall be weeping and gnashing of teeth.

25 ¹Then shall the kingdom of heaven be likened unto ten virgins, which took their lamps, and went forth to meet the bridegroom. ²And five of them were wise, and five were foolish. ³They that were foolish took their lamps, and took no oil with them, ⁴but the wise took oil in their vessels with their lamps. ⁵While the bridegroom tarried, they all slumbered and slept. ⁶And at midnight there was a cry made, "Behold, the bridegroom cometh; go ye out to meet him." ⁷Then all those virgins arose, and trimmed their lamps. ⁸And the foolish said unto the wise, "Give us of your oil; for our lamps are gone out." ⁹But the wise answered, saying, "Not so, lest there be not enough for us and you, but go ye rather to them that sell, and buy for yourselves." ¹⁰And while they went to buy, the bridegroom came; and they that were ready went in with him to the marriage; and the door was shut. ¹¹Afterward came also the other virgins, saying, "Lord, Lord, open to us." ¹²But he answered and said, "Verily I say unto you, I know you not." ¹³Watch therefore, for ye know neither the day nor the hour wherein the Son of man cometh.

¹⁴'For the kingdom of heaven is as a man travelling into a far country, who called his own servants, and delivered unto them his goods, ¹⁵and unto one he gave five talents, to another two, and to another one; to every man according to his several ability; and straightway took his journey. ¹⁶Then he that had received the five talents went and traded with the same,

and made them other five talents. ¹⁷And likewise he that had received two, he also gained other two. ¹⁸But he that had received one went and digged in the earth, and hid his lord's money. ¹⁹After a long time the lord of those servants cometh, and reckoneth with them. ²⁰And so he that had received five talents came and brought other five talents, saying, "Lord, thou deliveredst unto me five talents; behold, I have gained beside them five talents more." ²¹His lord said unto him, "Well done, thou good and faithful servant: thou hast been faithful over a few things; I will make thee ruler over many things; enter thou into the joy of thy lord." ²²He also that had received two talents came and said, "Lord, thou deliveredst unto me two talents; behold, I have gained two other talents beside them." ²³His lord said unto him, "Well done, good and faithful servant; thou hast been faithful over a few things, I will make thee ruler over many things; enter thou into the joy of thy lord." ²⁴Then he which had received the one talent came and said, "Lord, I knew thee that thou art an hard man, reaping where thou hast not sown, and gathering where thou hast not strawed, ²⁵and I was afraid, and went and hid thy talent in the earth: lo, there thou hast that is thine." ²⁶His lord answered and said unto him, "Thou wicked and slothful servant, thou knewest that I reap where I sowed not, and gather where I have not strawed. ²⁷Thou oughtest therefore to have put my money to the exchangers, and then at my coming I should have received mine own with usury. ²⁸Take therefore the talent from him, and give it unto him which hath ten talents. ²⁹For unto every one that hath shall be given, and he shall have abundance: but from him that hath not shall be taken away even that which he hath. ³⁰And cast ye the unprofitable servant into outer darkness: there shall be weeping and gnashing of teeth."

³¹'When the Son of man shall come in his glory, and all the holy angels with him, then shall he sit upon the throne of his glory, ³²and before him shall be gathered all nations, and he shall separate them one from another, as a shepherd divideth his sheep from the goats, ³³and he shall set the sheep on his right hand, but the goats on the left. ³⁴Then shall the King say unto them on his right hand, "Come, ye blessed of my Father, inherit the kingdom prepared for you from the foundation of the world; ³⁵for I was an hungred, and ye gave me meat; I was thirsty, and ye gave me drink; I was a stranger, and ye took me in; ³⁶naked, and ye clothed me; I was sick, and ye visited me; I was in prison, and ye came unto me." ³⁷Then shall the righteous answer him, saying, "Lord, when saw we thee an hungred, and fed thee? Or thirsty, and gave thee drink? ³⁸When saw we thee a stranger, and took thee in? Or naked, and clothed thee? ³⁹Or when saw we thee sick, or in prison, and came unto thee?" ⁴⁰And the King shall answer and say unto them, "Verily I say unto you, inasmuch as ye have done it unto one of the least of these my brethren, ye have done it unto me." ⁴¹Then shall he say also unto them on the left hand, "Depart from me, ye cursed, into everlasting fire, prepared for the devil and his angels: ⁴²for I was an hungred, and ye gave me no meat; I was thirsty, and ye gave me no drink; ⁴³I was a stranger, and ye took me not in; naked, and ye clothed me not; sick, and in prison, and ye visited me not." ⁴⁴Then shall they also answer him, saying, "Lord, when

saw we thee an hungred, or athirst, or a stranger, or naked, or sick, or in prison, and did not minister unto thee?" ⁴⁵Then shall he answer them, saying, "Verily I say unto you, inasmuch as ye did it not to one of the least of these, ye did it not to me." ⁴⁶And these shall go away into everlasting punishment, but the righteous into life eternal.'

26 And it came to pass, when Jesus had finished all these sayings, he said unto his disciples, ²'Ye know that after two days is the feast of the passover, and the Son of man is betrayed to be crucified.' ³Then assembled together the chief priests, and the scribes, and the elders of the people, unto the palace of the high priest, who was called Caiaphas, ⁴and consulted that they might take Jesus by subtilty, and kill him. ⁵But they said, 'Not on the feast day, lest there be an uproar among the people.'

⁶Now when Jesus was in Bethany, in the house of Simon the leper, ⁷there came unto him a woman having an alabaster box of very precious ointment, and poured it on his head, as he sat at meat. ⁸But when his disciples saw it, they had indignation, saying, 'To what purpose is this waste? ⁹For this ointment might have been sold for much, and given to the poor.' ¹⁰When Jesus understood it, he said unto them, 'Why trouble ye the woman? For she hath wrought a good work upon me. ¹¹For ye have the poor always with you; but me ye have not always. ¹²For in that she hath poured this ointment on my body, she did it for my burial. ¹³Verily I say unto you, wheresoever this gospel shall be preached in the whole world, there shall also this, that this woman hath

done, be told for a memorial of her.'

¹⁴ Then one of the twelve, called Judas Iscariot, went unto the chief priests, ¹⁵ and said unto them, 'What will ye give me, and I will deliver him unto you?' And they covenanted with him for thirty pieces of silver. ¹⁶ And from that time he sought opportunity to betray him.

¹⁷ Now the first day of the feast of unleavened bread the disciples came to Jesus, saying unto him, 'Where wilt thou that we prepare for thee to eat the passover?' ¹⁸ And he said, 'Go into the city to such a man, and say unto him, "The Master saith, 'My time is at hand; I will keep the passover at thy house with my disciples.'"' ¹⁹ And the disciples did as Jesus had appointed them; and they made ready the passover. ²⁰ Now when the even was come, he sat down with the twelve. ²¹ And as they did eat, he said, 'Verily I say unto you that one of you shall betray me.' ²² And they were exceeding sorrowful, and began every one of them to say unto him, 'Lord, is it I?' ²³ And he answered and said, 'He that dippeth his hand with me in the dish, the same shall betray me. ²⁴ The Son of man goeth as it is written of him, but woe unto that man by whom the Son of man is betrayed! It had been good for that man if he had not been born.' ²⁵ Then Judas, which betrayed him, answered and said, 'Master, is it I?' He said unto him, 'Thou hast said.'

²⁶ And as they were eating, Jesus took bread, and blessed it, and brake it, and gave it to the disciples, and said, 'Take, eat; this is my body.' ²⁷ And he took the cup, and gave thanks, and gave it to them, saying, 'Drink ye all of it, ²⁸ for this is my blood of the new testament, which is shed for many for the

remission of sins. [29] But I say unto you, I will not drink henceforth of this fruit of the vine, until that day when I drink it new with you in my Father's kingdom.' [30] And when they had sung an hymn, they went out into the mount of Olives. [31] Then saith Jesus unto them, 'All ye shall be offended because of me this night, for it is written, "I will smite the shepherd, and the sheep of the flock shall be scattered abroad." [32] But after I am risen again, I will go before you into Galilee.' [33] Peter answered and said unto him, 'Though all men shall be offended because of thee, yet will I never be offended.' [34] Jesus said unto him, 'Verily I say unto thee that this night, before the cock crow, thou shalt deny me thrice.' [35] Peter said unto him, 'Though I should die with thee, yet will I not deny thee.' Likewise also said all the disciples.

[36] Then cometh Jesus with them unto a place called Gethsemane, and saith unto the disciples, 'Sit ye here, while I go and pray yonder.' [37] And he took with him Peter and the two sons of Zebedee, and began to be sorrowful and very heavy. [38] Then saith he unto them, 'My soul is exceeding sorrowful, even unto death; tarry ye here, and watch with me.' [39] And he went a little farther, and fell on his face, and prayed, saying, 'O my Father, if it be possible, let this cup pass from me: nevertheless not as I will, but as thou wilt.' [40] And he cometh unto the disciples, and findeth them asleep, and saith unto Peter, 'What, could ye not watch with me one hour? [41] Watch and pray, that ye enter not into temptation: the spirit indeed is willing, but the flesh is weak.' [42] He went away again the second time, and prayed, saying, 'O my Father, if this cup may not pass away from me, except I drink it, thy will be

done.' ⁴³And he came and found them asleep again: for their eyes were heavy. ⁴⁴And he left them, and went away again, and prayed the third time, saying the same words. ⁴⁵Then cometh he to his disciples, and saith unto them, 'Sleep on now, and take your rest: behold, the hour is at hand, and the Son of man is betrayed into the hands of sinners. ⁴⁶Rise, let us be going: behold, he is at hand that doth betray me.'

⁴⁷And while he yet spake, lo, Judas, one of the twelve, came, and with him a great multitude with swords and staves, from the chief priests and elders of the people. ⁴⁸Now he that betrayed him gave them a sign, saying, 'Whomsoever I shall kiss, that same is he; hold him fast.' ⁴⁹And forthwith he came to Jesus, and said, 'Hail, master,' and kissed him. ⁵⁰And Jesus said unto him, 'Friend, wherefore art thou come?' Then came they, and laid hands on Jesus, and took him. ⁵¹And, behold, one of them which were with Jesus stretched out his hand, and drew his sword, and struck a servant of the high priest's, and smote off his ear. ⁵²Then said Jesus unto him, 'Put up again thy sword into his place: for all they that take the sword shall perish with the sword. ⁵³Thinkest thou that I cannot now pray to my Father, and he shall presently give me more than twelve legions of angels? ⁵⁴But how then shall the scriptures be fulfilled, that thus it must be?' ⁵⁵In that same hour said Jesus to the multitudes, 'Are ye come out as against a thief with swords and staves for to take me? I sat daily with you teaching in the temple, and ye laid no hold on me. ⁵⁶But all this was done, that the scriptures of the prophets might be fulfilled.' Then all the disciples forsook him, and fled.

⁵⁷And they that had laid hold on Jesus led him away to Caiaphas the high priest, where the scribes and the elders were assembled. ⁵⁸But Peter followed him afar off unto the high priest's palace, and went in, and sat with the servants, to see the end. ⁵⁹Now the chief priests, and elders, and all the council, sought false witness against Jesus, to put him to death, ⁶⁰but found none; yea, though many false witnesses came, yet found they none. At the last came two false witnesses, ⁶¹and said, 'This fellow said, "I am able to destroy the temple of God, and to build it in three days."' ⁶²And the high priest arose, and said unto him, 'Answerest thou nothing? What is it which these witness against thee?' ⁶³But Jesus held his peace. And the high priest answered and said unto him, 'I adjure thee by the living God, that thou tell us whether thou be the Christ, the Son of God.' ⁶⁴Jesus saith unto him, 'Thou hast said: nevertheless I say unto you, hereafter shall ye see the Son of man sitting on the right hand of power, and coming in the clouds of heaven.' ⁶⁵Then the high priest rent his clothes, saying, 'He hath spoken blasphemy; what further need have we of witnesses? Behold, now ye have heard his blasphemy. ⁶⁶What think ye?' They answered and said, 'He is guilty of death.' ⁶⁷Then did they spit in his face, and buffeted him; and others smote him with the palms of their hands, ⁶⁸saying, 'Prophesy unto us, thou Christ. Who is he that smote thee?'

⁶⁹Now Peter sat without in the palace, and a damsel came unto him, saying, 'Thou also wast with Jesus of Galilee.' ⁷⁰But he denied before them all, saying, 'I know not what thou sayest.' ⁷¹And when he was gone out into the porch,

another maid saw him, and said unto them that were there, 'This fellow was also with Jesus of Nazareth.' [72]And again he denied with an oath: 'I do not know the man.' [73]And after a while came unto him they that stood by, and said to Peter, 'Surely thou also art one of them; for thy speech bewrayeth thee.' [74]Then began he to curse and to swear, saying, 'I know not the man.' And immediately the cock crew. [75]And Peter remembered the word of Jesus, which said unto him, 'Before the cock crow, thou shalt deny me thrice.' And he went out, and wept bitterly.

27 When the morning was come, all the chief priests and elders of the people took counsel against Jesus to put him to death: [2]and when they had bound him, they led him away, and delivered him to Pontius Pilate the governor.

[3]Then Judas, which had betrayed him, when he saw that he was condemned, repented himself, and brought again the thirty pieces of silver to the chief priests and elders, [4]saying, 'I have sinned in that I have betrayed the innocent blood.' And they said, 'What is that to us? See thou to that.' [5]And he cast down the pieces of silver in the temple, and departed, and went and hanged himself. [6]And the chief priests took the silver pieces, and said, 'It is not lawful for to put them into the treasury, because it is the price of blood.' [7]And they took counsel, and bought with them the potter's field, to bury strangers in. [8]Wherefore that field was called 'the field of blood' unto this day. [9]Then was fulfilled that which was spoken by Jeremy the prophet, saying, 'And they took the thirty pieces of silver, the price of him that was valued,

whom they of the children of Israel did value, ¹⁰and gave them for the potter's field, as the Lord appointed me.' ¹¹And Jesus stood before the governor, and the governor asked him, saying, 'Art thou the King of the Jews?' And Jesus said unto him, 'Thou sayest.' ¹²And when he was accused of the chief priests and elders, he answered nothing. ¹³Then said Pilate unto him, 'Hearest thou not how many things they witness against thee?' ¹⁴And he answered him to never a word; insomuch that the governor marvelled greatly. ¹⁵Now at that feast the governor was wont to release unto the people a prisoner, whom they would. ¹⁶And they had then a notable prisoner, called Barabbas. ¹⁷Therefore when they were gathered together, Pilate said unto them, 'Whom will ye that I release unto you? Barabbas, or Jesus which is called Christ?' ¹⁸For he knew that for envy they had delivered him.

¹⁹When he was set down on the judgment seat, his wife sent unto him, saying, 'Have thou nothing to do with that just man: for I have suffered many things this day in a dream because of him.' ²⁰But the chief priests and elders persuaded the multitude that they should ask Barabbas, and destroy Jesus. ²¹The governor answered and said unto them, 'Whether of the twain will ye that I release unto you?' They said, 'Barabbas.' ²²Pilate saith unto them, 'What shall I do then with Jesus which is called Christ?' They all say unto him, 'Let him be crucified.' ²³And the governor said, 'Why, what evil hath he done?' But they cried out the more, saying, 'Let him be crucified.'

²⁴When Pilate saw that he could prevail nothing, but that rather a tumult was made, he took water, and washed his

hands before the multitude, saying, 'I am innocent of the blood of this just person: see ye to it.' ²⁵ Then answered all the people, and said, 'His blood be on us, and on our children.'

²⁶ Then released he Barabbas unto them, and when he had scourged Jesus, he delivered him to be crucified. ²⁷ Then the soldiers of the governor took Jesus into the common hall, and gathered unto him the whole band of soldiers. ²⁸ And they stripped him, and put on him a scarlet robe.

²⁹ And when they had platted a crown of thorns, they put it upon his head, and a reed in his right hand, and they bowed the knee before him, and mocked him, saying, 'Hail, King of the Jews!' ³⁰ And they spit upon him, and took the reed, and smote him on the head. ³¹ And after that they had mocked him, they took the robe off from him, and put his own raiment on him, and led him away to crucify him. ³² And as they came out, they found a man of Cyrene, Simon by name: him they compelled to bear his cross. ³³ And when they were come unto a place called Golgotha, that is to say, a place of a skull, ³⁴ they gave him vinegar to drink mingled with gall, and when he had tasted thereof, he would not drink. ³⁵ And they crucified him, and parted his garments, casting lots: that it might be fulfilled which was spoken by the prophet, 'They parted my garments among them, and upon my vesture did they cast lots.' ³⁶ And sitting down they watched him there; ³⁷ and set up over his head his accusation written, 'This is Jesus the King of the Jews.' ³⁸ Then were there two thieves crucified with him, one on the right hand, and another on the left.

³⁹ And they that passed by reviled him, wagging their

heads, ⁴⁰and saying, 'Thou that destroyest the temple, and buildest it in three days, save thyself. If thou be the Son of God, come down from the cross.' ⁴¹Likewise also the chief priests, mocking him, with the scribes and elders, said, ⁴²'He saved others; himself he cannot save. If he be the King of Israel, let him now come down from the cross, and we will believe him. ⁴³He trusted in God; let him deliver him now, if he will have him: for he said, "I am the Son of God."' ⁴⁴The thieves also, which were crucified with him, cast the same in his teeth. ⁴⁵Now from the sixth hour there was darkness over all the land unto the ninth hour. ⁴⁶And about the ninth hour Jesus cried with a loud voice, saying, 'Eli, Eli, lama sabachthani?' that is to say, 'My God, my God, why hast thou forsaken me?' ⁴⁷Some of them that stood there, when they heard that, said, 'This man calleth for Elias.' ⁴⁸And straightway one of them ran, and took a spunge, and filled it with vinegar, and put it on a reed, and gave him to drink. ⁴⁹The rest said, 'Let be, let us see whether Elias will come to save him.'

⁵⁰Jesus, when he had cried again with a loud voice, yielded up the ghost. ⁵¹And, behold, the veil of the temple was rent in twain from the top to the bottom; and the earth did quake, and the rocks rent; ⁵²and the graves were opened; and many bodies of the saints which slept arose, ⁵³and came out of the graves after his resurrection, and went into the holy city, and appeared unto many. ⁵⁴Now when the centurion, and they that were with him, watching Jesus, saw the earthquake, and those things that were done, they feared greatly, saying, 'Truly this was the Son of God.' ⁵⁵And many women were there beholding afar off, which followed Jesus from Galilee,

ministering unto him, ⁵⁶ among which was Mary Magdalene, and Mary the mother of James and Joses, and the mother of Zebedee's children. ⁵⁷ When the even was come, there came a rich man of Arimathæa, named Joseph, who also himself was Jesus' disciple. ⁵⁸ He went to Pilate, and begged the body of Jesus. Then Pilate commanded the body to be delivered. ⁵⁹And when Joseph had taken the body, he wrapped it in a clean linen cloth, ⁶⁰ and laid it in his own new tomb, which he had hewn out in the rock, and he rolled a great stone to the door of the sepulchre, and departed. ⁶¹And there was Mary Magdalene, and the other Mary, sitting over against the sepulchre.

⁶² Now the next day, that followed the day of the preparation, the chief priests and Pharisees came together unto Pilate, ⁶³ saying, 'Sir, we remember that that deceiver said, while he was yet alive, "After three days I will rise again." ⁶⁴ Command therefore that the sepulchre be made sure until the third day, lest his disciples come by night, and steal him away, and say unto the people, "He is risen from the dead," so the last error shall be worse than the first.' ⁶⁵ Pilate said unto them, 'Ye have a watch: go your way, make it as sure as ye can.' ⁶⁶ So they went, and made the sepulchre sure, sealing the stone, and setting a watch.

28

In the end of the sabbath, as it began to dawn toward the first day of the week, came Mary Magdalene and the other Mary to see the sepulchre. ²And, behold, there was a great earthquake: for the angel of the Lord descended from heaven, and came and rolled back the stone from the door, and sat upon it. ³His countenance was like lightning, and his raiment white as snow, ⁴and for fear of him the keepers did shake, and became as dead men. ⁵And the angel answered and said unto the women, 'Fear not ye, for I know that ye seek Jesus, which was crucified. ⁶He is not here: for he is risen, as he said. Come, see the place where the Lord lay. ⁷And go quickly, and tell his disciples that he is risen from the dead; and, behold, he goeth before you into Galilee; there shall ye see him: lo, I have told you.' ⁸And they departed quickly from the sepulchre with fear and great joy; and did run to bring his disciples word.

⁹And as they went to tell his disciples, behold, Jesus met them, saying, 'All hail.' And they came and held him by the feet, and worshipped him. ¹⁰Then said Jesus unto them, 'Be not afraid: go tell my brethren that they go into Galilee, and there shall they see me.'

¹¹Now when they were going, behold, some of the watch came into the city, and shewed unto the chief priests all the things that were done. ¹²And when they were assembled with the elders, and had taken counsel, they gave large money unto the soldiers, ¹³saying, 'Say ye, "His disciples came by night, and stole him away while we slept." ¹⁴And if this come to the governor's ears, we will persuade him, and secure you.' ¹⁵So they took the money, and did as they were taught, and this saying is commonly reported among the Jews until this day.

¹⁶Then the eleven disciples went away into Galilee, into a mountain where Jesus had appointed them. ¹⁷And when they saw him, they worshipped him, but some doubted. ¹⁸And Jesus came and spake unto them, saying, 'All power is

given unto me in heaven and in earth.

¹⁹ 'Go ye therefore, and teach all nations, baptizing them in the name of the Father, and of the Son, and of the Holy Ghost, ²⁰ teaching them to observe all things whatsoever I have commanded you, and, lo, I am with you alway, even unto the end of the world. Amen.'

titles in the series

genesis – *introduced by steven rose*
exodus – *introduced by david grossman*
job – *introduced by louis de bernières*
proverbs – *introduced by charles johnson*
ecclesiastes – *introduced by doris lessing*
song of solomon – *introduced by a s byatt*
matthew – *introduced by a n wilson*
mark – *introduced by nick cave*
luke – *introduced by richard holloway*
john – *introduced by blake morrison*
corinthians – *introduced by fay weldon*
revelation – *introduced by will self*